BELIEVE
AND
REJOICE

BELIEVE AND REJOICE

JAMES P. GILLS, M.D.

**CREATION
HOUSE**

This book is dedicated to all those who will grasp the inner joy that comes from receiving the love of God by faith and relinquishing themselves to God. Our daughters are named Joy, Peace (Shea), and Charity. This book is dedicated to those three names and those three people. A relinquished life lives upon the faithful promises of God. The result is His joy, His peace, and His charity. Our daughters' names are symbols of the results of a relinquished life that believes totally in the promises of God.

To this we dedicate all our labors: to the future generations that will follow Him with a relinquished dependence on His faithfulness, trusting in His grace for an outpouring of joy, peace, and charity.

I want to express a special word of appreciation for my daughter-in-law, Joy Gills, for her insightful comments in the revised edition of *Believe and Rejoice*. Joy, we want to give the Spirit of God the glory for working the fruit of joy in your life and in ours and in those who read this book.

—*JAMES P. GILLS AND GARY CARTER*

Now may the God of hope fill you with all joy and peace in believing, that you may abound in hope by the power of the Holy Spirit.

—*ROMANS 15:13, NKJV*

ACKNOWLEDGMENTS

This book would not have been possible without my good friend and colleague at St. Luke's, Gary Carter. Gary and I have spent countless hours studying, discussing, praying, and fellowshiping over God's Word and its meaning in our lives. Gary is truly filled with faith in God's promises, and I am blessed to share in his life of joy.

I would also like to thank the staff members at St. Luke's Cataract & Laser Institute, especially Lois Babcock, for generously providing their encouragement and direction, and Victoria Krueger for her editing assistance.

And finally, my thanks to my wife, Heather. Her love and insight continue to be a source of inspiration to me.

CONTENTS

Introduction   ix

1   *A Heart of Faith, a Life of Joy*   1

2   *The Joy of Salvation*   5

3   *Being Relinquished*   10

4   *Traits of a Relinquished Life*   26

5   *The Struggle to Stay Relinquished*   35

6   *Relinquished or Religious?*   50

7   *Restored to Joy*   59

8   *Worship and Joy*   64

9   *A Joyous Life*   79

10   *Joy and Peace*   86

Verses About Joy   93

Verses About Worship   96

Relinquished Heart or Religious Spirit?   99

Sara Edwards, A Model of Relinquished Joy   107

Scripture Index   113

Notes   115

INTRODUCTION

During an interesting part of my life in which there were a lot of temptations and trials, I read a short book by the Reverend Henry Scougal called *The Life of God in the Soul of Man*.[1] I read this book ten times, because it meant so much to me during that time. Each time I read it, its message became more and more meaningful.

This book showed me how my life can be filled with joy. All I had to do was really believe in God, always be dependent on Him, and always worship Him. Then my trials and temptations would be overshadowed by His love for me and my joy in resting in Him. John 3:16 shows us why we can rest in God's redemptive love: "For God so loved the world that He gave His only begotten Son, that whoever believes in Him should not perish but have everlasting life" (NKJV). This verse is simply saying that God loves us, He is the One who saves us, and we must rest in that and live. That's the essence of the Christian walk. Oswald Chambers said that all prayer that isn't based on resting in His redemption is foolishness.[2]

The psalmist explains it so beautifully this way:

> Whom have I in heaven but you? And earth has nothing I desire besides you. My flesh and my heart may fail, but God is the strength of my heart and my portion forever.
> —PSALM 73:25–26

In the final analysis, we have no one but our Creator-Redeemer, the Lord God, and He is all we will ever need. The God who set the universe in motion also concerns Himself with the daily needs in each of our lives. And all we have to do is trust in the Savior's work on the cross, embrace His control of our lives, acknowledge His majesty and greatness, believe in His promises, and live in a loving relationship with Him. In that relationship shall we find joy.

Communion with the risen Lord is our daily joy; this is the source of our strength in all that we do. How can we be anything but joyful when we experience a close relationship with the Creator of the universe, enjoying His peace and presence forever? For when we believe in Him and surrender ourselves to His will, we are filled with a joyful spirit. We must do all the things we do because of having received God's love, not in order to obtain God's love. Then there will be a natural outpouring of joy.

> These things I have spoken to you, that My joy may remain in you, and that your joy may be full.
> —JOHN 15:11, NKJV

> As the Father loved Me, I also have loved you; abide in My love.
> —JOHN 15:9, NKJV

We must abide in His love and do everything because God loves us. This is set before us in that wonderful passage, Ephesians 3:17–19 (NKJV):

> That Christ may dwell in your hearts through faith; that you, being rooted and grounded in love, may be able to comprehend with all the saints what is the width and length and depth and height—to know the love of Christ which passes knowledge; that you may be filled with all the fullness of God.

The Reverend Scougal wrote that we cannot have this true joy of God until we have surrendered everything—our wants, our desires, our anger, our resentment, and our bitterness—to

Him.[3] Eighteenth-century theologian and evangelist Jonathan Edwards described this surrender as the "religious affections" of grace.[4] By that, he meant that we are not just surrendered; our hearts are engaged fervently in praising and worshiping God, because His Word has come to us with power, and we believe in Him.

The Bible teaches us that He wants our praise, because we have received His salvation, and we enjoy His fellowship. And then we are transformed. When we are filled with these "holy affections," life is no longer an endless search for meaning. We surrender ourselves, putting the focus of our lives on God and on worshiping Him. We are filled with the presence of God. Indeed, we must relinquish ourselves to God in faith or we will never be able to worship and love Him fully. We will never have a completely joyous existence unless we worship Him with a heart that fervently believes in Him.

Believing God's promises, not just intellectually but also in the inner being, has transformed people and nations. That kind of belief grabs everything about us and changes our lives.

When we praise Him, we are filled with joy. That joy strengthens us in daily life, in our service, and in our work for God. When I do not have God's joy, the day is very long, and I am less effective. When I have His joy, the day is easy.

I have to examine myself daily and make sure I am receiving His Word and resting in His love. I trust in God and rest in His control of my life. I let my relationship with Him govern my life. I must rest in His presence, not wrestle with Him for control. Then, when my heart is given over to Him in faith, I am naturally filled with joy. This joy is not something I can produce myself. It happens only because He is at work in me, and I believe in Him. He is in charge, and our relationship is in order.

What all this means to me is that life is too short not to be full of joy! Life is too short to be jealous or envious of others.

It is too short to be angry or resentful. It is too short to carry a grudge. It is too short to worry about material goods and be caught up in the pursuit of status or possessions. It is too short to do anything other than trust in Him, worship Him, and let His joy fill my life.

Explore with me in this book how we can relinquish our hearts to God, believing in Him, worshiping Him, and enjoying Him forever—for a joy-filled life in Him!

1

A HEART OF FAITH,
A LIFE OF JOY

Glory in his holy name;
let the hearts of those who seek the Lord rejoice.
—1 Chronicles 16:10

Think about the word *joy*. What image comes to mind? Angels in the heavens announcing the birth of Christ? A child full of laughter and happiness? Beethoven's beautiful ninth symphony? Nineteenth-century preacher C. H. Spurgeon said, "Joy is peace dancing."[1] What a wonderful image!

God wants us to have a life filled with more joy than we can ever imagine. It doesn't happen by accident, but it does surprise us. Author C. S. Lewis wrote that we find joy only when we are looking for something else.[2] And that something else is God. It is a one-two punch: we seek God, really believing in Him, and we find joy. Lewis said it more eloquently: joy is the response or result of the felt sense of God's love in our soul.

It is a journey we undertake when we turn our lives over to God. When we truly believe in God, we surrender every worry, every concern, and every aspect of our lives to Him. We are concerned only about living in God's presence and believing in His promises.

The apostle Paul described three critical elements in this journey to a joy-filled life: relinquishment, faith, and grace.

> I have been crucified with Christ and I no longer live, but Christ lives in me. The life I live in the body, I live by faith in the Son of God, who loved me and gave himself for me.
> —GALATIANS 2:20

Sometimes we are reluctant to talk about joy and God. We tend to associate joy with comfort, ease, and luxury. But joy is a much deeper and richer experience. It is the natural outpouring of our hearts as God's presence becomes the central pillar of our lives. When we have a personal relationship with Him, we cannot help but be filled with heavenly, glorious joy and the desire to worship and adore God. His full presence in our lives is the ultimate joy.

How do we get that kind of personal relationship? First, we have to acknowledge God as our Creator. Then we have to really believe in Him as our Savior. We have to love Him and trust Him enough to embrace His rule over our lives. There is an old-fashioned word to describe it—*relinquishment*. The dictionary says that to relinquish means "to abandon, surrender, let go."[3] When we are passengers in a car, we have to relinquish control to the person behind the wheel or we take the terrible role of backseat drivers.

Relinquishment is a combination of surrendering and entrusting yourself to God. *Surrender* is the parallel of repentance and *entrusting yourself* is a way of expressing faith. The apostle Paul summarized his teaching of the whole counsel of God in these words: "repentance toward God and faith toward our Lord Jesus Christ" (Acts 20:21, NKJV).

For Christians, relinquishing means surrendering our lives,

giving up our wants and desires, cares and worries, abandoning our selfish nature, receiving God's love, trusting His provision, and experiencing His filling. Our faith helps us leave behind all the cares and concerns of this world. We can call it "abandoned faith" because we are abandoning the world for a life of faith in God. We are filled with trust in God, and we relinquish control to Him. And then we are filled with abundant, glorious joy.

The experience of John Wesley, the great evangelist and founder of the Methodist movement, shows how abandoned faith can change a life. By the time he was thirty-five, Wesley knew a lot about Christ. He had graduated from Oxford University and resolved to become a priest in the Church of England. He was ordained a priest in 1728. He and his brother, Charles, helped start the Holy Club at Oxford. He read one hundred spiritual books a year for a dozen years. He even traveled to Georgia on a mission trip. But he knew there was something missing. On his mission trip he met some Moravian immigrants who had the spiritual peace he realized he was lacking. His work in America was not very effective, and he returned to England.

Back in London, Wesley met Peter Böhler, a Moravian who convinced him that what he needed was simple: he needed faith, not just knowledge. During a meeting in Aldersgate Street in 1738, Wesley was transformed. As he heard Martin Luther's preface to the Commentary on Romans being read, he was truly elated. He realized the promises of God are true! He wrote, "I felt my heart strangely warmed. I felt I did trust in Christ, Christ alone, for salvation."[4] He felt a quickening that comes from truly experiencing God's grace and presence. He was filled with God's complete and perfect joy.

From this point on, Wesley was a changed man. He preached with a spiritual fire and fervor that was fed by his faith. And he was filled with a glorious joy that affected him the rest of his life because he was relinquished to God and believed in His promises.

We can have the same kind of life filled with abandoned faith and joy. It's a faith and joy that comes from inner harmony. We experience a victorious counteraction to our internal struggles. And we learn the futility of complaining about trouble and worrying about trying to control the future. When we believe in God's promises and trust Him to be in control of our lives, joy is the glorious result. We do not have joy; it has us. Our joy in God is based on His delight in us. (See Ps. 149:4.)

What an offer! If we quit worrying about our own lives and trust God to do the driving, we will find our lives full of blessings and riches beyond our wildest dreams. Indeed, we cannot even begin to know all the blessings we will receive. And we limit God when we try.

> Indeed, if we consider the unblushing promises of reward and the staggering nature of the rewards promised in the Gospels, it would seem that Our Lord finds our desires not too strong, but too weak. We are half-hearted creatures, fooling about with drink and sex and ambition when infinite joy is offered us, like an ignorant child who wants to go on making mud pies in a slum because he cannot imagine what is meant by the offer of a holiday at the sea. We are far too easily pleased.[5]

In this study, through our reading, exploration of the Word, and prayer together, that is what we will find—the infinite, glorious joy that results from believing in God.

Dear Lord Jesus, bless us as we discover Your truths and learn to love You as You love us.

2

THE JOY OF SALVATION

The LORD your God is with you, he is mighty to save.
He will take great delight in you, he will quiet you
with his love, he will rejoice over you with singing.
—Zephaniah 3:17

Each of us has struggled to find joy, thinking the "right" thing in our work, our play, or our relationships will fulfill us. We create such hectic days full of activities and accomplishments that we think a filled life is a fulfilled life. We seek recreations on a basketball court, a gym, or a bicycle that engage us for the moment but are not lasting. Or we search for that "special someone," only to discover that our problem is not in finding the right person, but that we are not the right person ourselves.

C. S. Lewis said that each of us has this kind of deep longing that we search to fill. He calls it *sehnsucht* or "longing for joy."[1] Because we are human, we try to fill it with earthly things.

We say, "If I can just get my education finished and get started in my career, then things will go well and I will be happy." But we are not happy. So we say, "If I can just get established in my business and be successful, then things will go well and I will be happy." But it doesn't happen. Then we think, "Well, if I can just find the right spouse and have good children, then things will go well and I will be happy." But that still doesn't satisfy us. So then we say, "If I can just get the kids through school, then I can settle down and rest." But we are missing the point.

There are no magic plateaus where our lives level off and we think we have achieved happiness. Personal achievements, success at work or on the athletic field, and relationships cannot give us lasting joy. We can have all those things and still feel this empty longing.

At some point in our lives we have to realize that what we seek isn't within ourselves; we lack the inner resources to fill this void. We finally see how weak we are, how limited are our powers. We can be eaten up with despair, frustration, anger, anxiety, and loneliness.

Then God speaks to us. For the first time, we truly begin to see the power and majesty of the almighty God. We see ourselves as poor, needy sinners who need the grace of the Lord Jesus and His cross. We turn to God because we realize we have nowhere else to go.

> For it is by grace you have been saved, through faith—and this is not from yourselves, it is the gift of God—not by works, so that no one can boast.
>
> —EPHESIANS 2:8–9

Paul tells us in these verses, first, that it is only God's grace that can save us. And then God has a plan for our lives—as a physician or nurse, a teacher, a mechanic, a firefighter, a politician, a husband, or a wife. Paul continues: "For we are His workmanship, created in Christ Jesus for good works, which God prepared beforehand that we should walk in them" (Eph. 2:10, NKJV).

Our concept of grace varies immensely with our experiences over the course of our lives. We never quite fully understand God's divine grace. But we do delight in it; we cry over it; we laugh over it; and we worship over it.

Grace is a biblical word that can be the greatest word you hear or the word you let pass by without interest. If you are self-sufficient, proud, and self-righteous, you do not think you need God's grace. On the other hand, if you feel humbled or even humiliated because of your failings—your sins—you may hesitate to believe that there is a possibility of grace for your life. Jonathan Edwards understood this human conflict and expressed it so beautifully:

> If you're a poor distressed sinner whose heart is ready to sink for fear that God never will have mercy on you, you need not be afraid to go to Christ, for fear that he is either unable or unwilling to help you. Here is a strong foundation, inexhaustible treasure, to answer the necessities of your poor soul, and here is infinite grace and gentleness to invite you to come boldly, poor unworthy fearful soul, to come into it.[2]

The apostle Paul was ashamed of how he tried to exterminate Christians before his conversion, but the grace of God even changed Paul and gave him the joy of forgiveness. He described the grace of God working in his life:

> For I am the least of the apostles, who am not worthy to be called an apostle, because I persecuted the church of God. But by the grace of God I am what I am.
> —*1 CORINTHIANS 15:9–10, NKJV*

Paul called himself the chief of sinners (1 Tim. 1:15), and felt he was less than the least of the saints. (See Eph. 3:8.) He was amazed that God would graciously forgive all of his sins because of what Jesus did on the cross to save him. Yet, he did believe the good news of the gospel and gave his life to spread that good news to others. The Philippian jailer probably felt there was little hope for him as an enemy of God's apostles, roughly throwing them into the inner prison and putting them into stocks. Yet, Paul boldly proclaimed to him: "Believe on the Lord Jesus Christ, and you will be saved" (Acts 16:31, NKJV).

This same promise is true for you and me. Let us cast ourselves upon God's mercy and grace. We will find that God delights to show mercy (see Mic. 7:18) and will forgive us and make us His own children. God says it! Let's believe it!

How gracious and sweet is God's invitation. We fall at His feet and say, *Lord, I'm a poor, worthless sinner. Please, in your everlasting mercy and grace, accept me, take me, let me be Yours. Be my Redeemer, Savior, and Friend, for I trust and believe in You and I love You.*

May God flood our souls with the joy of salvation. May we begin to see the infinite majesty of God. He has given us hope and joy in believing!

> Then my soul will rejoice in the LORD and delight in his salvation.
>
> —*PSALM 35:9*

Joy is a heart that is changed by knowing God. It takes our breath away. It is an infinite host of angels singing glory to God. It is the greatest music or words we can ever imagine, and still more. This great joy puts everything else out of our heads and our hearts. In turning from earthly things we find God. And by putting our faith in Him, we are filled with abundant joy.

If you have not received Jesus as your personal Savior and heavenly Friend, pray with me:

Lord, I realize how far short I have fallen. I know I'm not worthy of Your love. But, through the miracle of Your grace, forgive me and make me Your child. Help me turn to You and love You. Show me how to live and love and be like You.

3

BEING RELINQUISHED

We cannot have joy without love. It is like two people in love—joy springs up and fills them when they have an unconditional love for each other. That is the joy that should be our response to Christ—someone who loves us far more than anyone else ever could.

This new relationship has a wonderful sense of love and joy. The Bible calls it delight. "For the LORD takes delight in his people" (Ps. 149:4). God takes pleasure in us; we rejoice in that and take pleasure in Him. We are joyful in our King.

Love is essential to a life of faith and joy. God's Word tells us just how important it is:

> Love the LORD your God with all your heart and with all your soul and with all your strength.
> —DEUTERONOMY 6:5

For any of us, love must be a key step to a life that is surrendered in faith to God. Without love, our actions and words are meaningless. First Corinthians 13 says that we can have the gift of prophecy, understand all mysteries and knowledge, have faith to move mountains, give all our goods to the poor, and have our body burned. And we can have all sorts of abilities to speak, but unless we are relinquished in love to Christ and others, all these gifts and abilities do us no good. Churches or people who do not embrace love as Christ desires give Christianity a cold appearance.

As we tell God He is wonderful, we are in love with Him. It is like a marriage. As I tell my wife that she is wonderful, I am in love with her. Look at couples who struggle in their marriages. Insecurities, pride, hostility, and many other forms of selfishness keep them from becoming close and surrendering to one another.

We have the same problems in our relationship with Christ. We all have anxieties, frustrations, and doubts. But God commands us to turn them over to Him. He calls us to love Him and be in communion with Him. A heart filled with love has less room for selfishness. As we love God more and more, we can relinquish ourselves more and more.

We need to be able to look up to Jesus by faith and say, "Jesus, You're wonderful. I love You and I am Your child—Your spiritual child; Your child for eternity."

SWEET SURRENDER

If we are really going to be committed to God, we have to be committed to living a life that honors Him. We have to be able to say, "Lord, You're in charge now. I put all my faith in You. You lead; I'll follow." We must give up our worldly agendas and desires and trust His control of our lives. Then we find joy not by worldly standards—success, fame, money, or power. We find it in the outpouring of the love of our Creator and Redeemer into our hearts. (See Rom. 5:5.) Then we pour out our love to Him.

Think about it again like a marriage. I love my wife. I want what she wants; I sacrifice for her. I surrender myself to the joy of knowing, caring for, and appreciating her. I love to pray with my wife. One verse we pray together repeats what Adam said of Eve: "This is now bone of my bones and flesh of my flesh" (Gen. 2:23). That helps us remember that we can't really become one person, one partnership living in harmony, until we relinquish ourselves.

And just as any of us surrender to our spouses, so we must surrender ourselves to our God. Surrendering to God, we become one with Him spiritually in heart and joyfully in reality!

We love and trust God so completely that we can surrender our lives to Him. Love gives us the strength and trust to turn everything over to Him. Remember Paul's road map in Galatians 2:20 for this journey: surrender, faith, and grace. Let's look again at this first part:

> I have been crucified with Christ and I no longer live, but Christ lives in me.

What Paul says so beautifully is that we cannot live in Christ until we are ready to die to self—our own wants, desires, and egos. Jesus says it this way:

> Then he said to them all: "If anyone would come after me, he must deny himself and take up his cross daily and follow me. For whoever wants to save his life will lose it, but whoever loses his life for me will save it."
>
> —LUKE 9:23–24

> I tell you the truth, unless a kernel of wheat falls to the ground and dies, it remains only a single seed. But if it dies, it produces many seeds. The man who loves his life will lose it, while the man who hates his life in this world will keep it for eternal life.
>
> —JOHN 12:24–25

Paul also writes about relinquishment:

> I die every day—I mean that, brothers—just as surely as I
> glory over you in Christ Jesus our Lord.
> —*1 CORINTHIANS 15:31*

> We always carry around in our body the death of Jesus, so
> that the life of Jesus may also be revealed in our body.
> —*2 CORINTHIANS 4:10*

We must die to ourselves before we can truly appreciate God. We must give up our egos and all that goes with them—pride and the desire for control, worldly status, and success. This is what it means to be born again of the Spirit. And we must follow the scriptural command to "present your bodies a living sacrifice, holy, acceptable to God, which is your reasonable service" (Rom. 12:1, NKJV). The world and all of its lures, temptations, and struggles must no longer have a controlling grip on our lives. We belong to God and He lives in us. The Bible warns us about the opposite attitude:

> Don't you know that friendship with the world is hatred
> toward God? Anyone who chooses to be a friend of the
> world becomes an enemy of God.
> —*JAMES 4:4*

Everybody knows you must take risks to be successful by earthly standards. What we risk in order to make anything of our lives spiritually is even greater. We have to risk worldly success, risk losing our feeling of independence, and risk giving up control of our lives. But what we gain is so great that the risks pale in comparison. Charles Swindoll asked, "Are you willing to risk as much to make a difference as you are willing to risk to make a dollar?"[1] To be truly relinquished we have to risk it all.

As the apostle Paul wrote:

Believe and Rejoice

I consider everything a loss compared to the surpassing greatness of knowing Christ Jesus my Lord, for whose sake I have lost all things. I consider them rubbish, that I may gain Christ and be found in him.

—PHILIPPIANS 3:8–9

Dear God, I love You so very much. Help me to lovingly surrender every area and aspect of my life to You, that I may honor and glorify Your name above all others.

Faith: The Sixth Sense

The life I live in the body, I live by faith in the Son of God.

—GALATIANS 2:20

Great athletes must forget about everything else so they can train and play wholeheartedly. If they worry about getting injured or worry about how other athletes are doing, they cannot perform well. They cannot focus.

That is the essence of abandoned faith to the Lord: giving everything wholeheartedly to Him—every worry, concern, desire, and goal. It is a faith that is not just in our minds; it is a faith that believes all the promises of God. We must have a total abandonment spiritually, totally trusting in the Lord. The joy in our hearts that comes from abandonment to Him keeps us from worrying about the cares of the day, the politics of the day, and the cynicism of the day. It lets us be concerned only about being totally abandoned and surrendered to the Lord.

The apostle Paul, Martin Luther, and John Wesley are just some of the great Christians who went through a time when they truly had to believe. They knew all about the promises of God. But they didn't know Him. Peter Böhler explained it so simply and beautifully to Wesley: "Preach faith until you have it." Believing is the essence.[2]

Let's look at the word *belief*. Hebrews 11:6 tells us to diligently seek God, emphasizing that belief isn't simply an intellectual exercise. Instead, we lean upon, abide in, draw strength from, and become one with belief, and we act the way we believe.

Faith is really a sixth sense. The first five senses—touch, taste, smell, hearing, and sight—are in carnal man. The sixth sense is in the spiritual man. The carnal man cannot appreciate faith any more than the sense of hearing appreciates the sense of smell. But the sixth sense is absolutely essential if we are going to live complete lives full of joy. In seeking God, faith is given to us as we hear His Word.

> Consequently, faith comes from hearing the message, and
> the message is heard through the word of Christ.
> —*ROMANS 10:17*

The battle we have with our carnal selves is won in our hearts with God when we believe in Him. Then we step into a life of faith. And when we fully believe in God and His promises, then we have an abandoned faith that focuses on God and forgets the world.

Look at the example of Robert Morrison. He was one of the first missionaries to China in the early 1800s. As he was sailing to China, the captain of the ship asked, rather sarcastically, "So, Mr. Morrison, you expect to make an impression on the great empire of China, do you?" Morrison replied, "No, I expect God will."[3] What a shining example of believing God's promises! Morrison served twenty-seven years in China, and he is considered the father of Protestant mission work there.

It doesn't take a great mind or years of education to have such abandoned faith. As the old hymn says, "Trust and obey, for there's no other way."[4] All each of us needs to do is trust in God and believe in His promises.

However, we can either believe in the right things or the

wrong things. What are some of those deceptions that we should not start believing? "Life should be fair." "My unhappiness is because of someone else." "My good is determined by what I can do." "Our marriage requires too much work; we must not be right for each other." We start believing there are certain things we can do or things we can own that will solve our problems and fill our longings. But when we start seeking things that are not focused on God, we no longer have abandoned faith in Him. Instead, we start to abandon our faith in His promises.

We need not be deceived by the difficult times in our lives. God promises to help us through them. All we need to believe is that His grace is sufficient and all our blessings come because we believe in Him.

Dear Father, thank You for being so good to me. May my faith and trust in You grow daily.

COMMUNION AND CONVERSATION

When we love God, we want to be in His presence, and we want to talk with Him and share ourselves with Him. Prayer is one way we can be in constant communion with Him. In prayer we make the nearest approach to God. It opens the inward thoughts of both God and man, and true intimacy is found. In true sincerity we must open our hearts to God in prayer: sometimes with thoughtful, eloquent prayers; sometimes with words that cannot be uttered; sometimes with thoughts that cannot be translated. And then our hearts and our total beings are surrendered in intimacy to Him.

Fervent and hearty prayer is necessary. All-day-long prayers are necessary. This life of prayer should be a state of meditation on the glory of God. We must have this kind of personal, vital relationship with Him. Otherwise Christianity becomes a joyless burden, and at the end of our lives we will regret that we didn't pray, because we didn't relinquish ourselves and have faith in His grace.

This intimacy through prayer leads to fulfillment of joy because prayer is the nerve center of our vital fellowship with Jesus. It brings us a life filled with deep, abiding joy. As 1 John 1:3–4 says, "Our fellowship is with the Father and with his Son, Jesus Christ. We write this to make our joy complete."

We measure fluids by gallons. Some measure a dog's value by its loyalty to its master. Others may measure a dog's value by how much an owner is willing to pay a veterinarian for the dog's health care. Scripture teaches us to measure ourselves spiritually by the quality of our prayer life. We can measure the quality of our prayer life by asking ourselves how genuinely we praise God, how intently we draw near to God, and how effectively we are being transformed into His image. (See 2 Cor. 3:18.)

We become like what we love and honor. One way to show our love and honor for God is through prayer. That life of communion with God gives us all we need—peace and joy—for today and for eternity.

Father, let me love You, and in love, surrender to You, to Your grace, to Your will, with the help of the Holy Spirit filling me with Your presence.

THE HELP OF THE HOLY SPIRIT

No matter how much we try to will ourselves to surrender everything to God, it is something we cannot do alone. In marriage our spouses help us. To be truly relinquished to God, we need the Holy Spirit working in us. C. H. Spurgeon said, "There are times when I've been a half-inch from heaven and you've been a half-inch from heaven."[5] The Holy Spirit makes that difference as we focus on Him and wait on Him for His

Spirit and His closeness. His *shekinah* glory, the manifested glory of God, fills us, displacing the rest of the world. Then we are able to empty ourselves of the world and He fills us with Himself.

Moses gives us a vivid example of a life filled with this kind of glory:

> When Moses came down from Mount Sinai with the two tablets of the Testimony in his hands, he was not aware that his face was radiant because he had spoken with the LORD. When Aaron and all the Israelites saw Moses, his face was radiant, and they were afraid to come near him. But Moses called to them; so Aaron and all the leaders of the community came back to him, and he spoke to them…When Moses finished speaking to them, he put a veil over his face. But whenever he entered the LORD's presence to speak with him, he removed the veil until he came out. And when he came out and told the Israelites what he had been commanded, they saw that his face was radiant. Then Moses would put the veil back over his face until he went in to speak with the LORD.
> —*EXODUS 34:29–31, 33–35*

Moses had that physical reflection of the shekinah glory because he was so close to the Lord that he radiated with the glory of the Lord. And those around him would be alarmed by the glorious radiance of the Lord's presence. The shekinah glory is not something just for Old Testament prophets, however. It is for all of us today as we seek His presence.

> For God, who said, "Let light shine out of darkness," made his light shine in our hearts to give us the light of the knowledge of the glory of God in the face of Christ.
> —*2 CORINTHIANS 4:6*

And that glory comes through the work of the Holy Spirit. John 1:4 says that in Jesus "was life, and that life was the light of men." So Jesus, as the Light of Life, through the Holy Spirit, gives light upon the holy things of God. The apostle Paul explained:

> But we all, with unveiled face, beholding as in a mirror the glory of the Lord, are being transformed into the same image from glory to glory, just as by the Spirit of the Lord.
> —*2 CORINTHIANS 3:18, NKJV*

We need to commune with God, Jesus, and the Holy Spirit, each distinctly and all wrapped together to give us the joy that results from being present with Him. Shekinah glory comes only when we have a relinquished spirit of repentance and faith that loves Him, delights in Him, and worships Him. Then His shekinah glory is present within us, radiating into us and out into the world.

I have worked with nurses who had an aura of radiance. They might not have said anything holy, but their lives were filled with the presence of the Holy Spirit. They were full of the love of God and were completely surrendered to Him, letting Him direct their lives. This spirit of joy, peace, and thanksgiving is truly a wonderful sight.

I have felt a similar glow in my life. I will first mention that I am not much of an athlete, but I did fairly well years ago at a double iron triathlon. At that time I was fifty-six. I came in one minute behind the first American, who was twenty-eight, finishing in about twenty-seven hours. I did it that day just by prayer. USA *Today* and other newspapers wrote about the event, but no one wrote that during the whole event I was in one of those glows that many of us experience. The presence and influence of the Holy Spirit throughout the race kept me going. I was at my peak through the whole event; I was never down. It probably was my best athletic achievement ever. And it was due not to my own strength, but to God. "The joy of the LORD is your strength" (Neh. 8:10)!

The Israelites discovered that truth in the Old Testament. When they came out of their captivity in Babylon, they had nothing but the Word of God. When they heard it, they understood it and went their way rejoicing. They understood that though they had no material goods, they should not grieve and mourn. To be in God's presence is joyous and completely filling. The Israelites restored the Feast of Tabernacles, a feast of thanksgiving that honors God as the host and the Israelites as the guests.

In the same way, we daily should come to the Word of God and rejoice in His presence because we have faith in Him and in His Spirit.

The radiance of the Holy Spirit lets everyone see that we are truly His. It enables us to reflect Christ and His love. We can be like the nurses with that holy aura. They don't need to speak. They just let the light of Christ shine in their lives. The Holy Spirit can permeate the lives of each of us, so we will think differently, act differently, and live differently.

We can describe the smile of God upon our hearts that allows us to speak His Word as a divine unction or fervor. This is God's holiness speaking through us. Jesus' disciples demonstrated this divine unction:

> And the disciples were filled with joy and with the Holy Spirit.
>
> —ACTS 13:52

The disciples were infused with this joy and the Holy Spirit because their hearts were joined to God and filled with His presence. A few verses earlier we learn that when the Gentiles heard the good news of the gospel, they rejoiced, praising and honoring the Word of God, and they were glorified. (See Acts 13:48.)

They were filled with joy because it came from the praise that the Holy Spirit stirred up within them And that praise changes our inner being and gives us true joy. When the Holy Spirit gives us His glory, we need to enjoy it and cherish it and tell Him how wonderful He is to give it to us.

Tony Evans describes the importance of the Holy Spirit in the believer's life in a surprising manner.[6] His analogy is jumper cables from Jesus to us. Can you imagine having jumper cables to use in the morning to get your mind turned on right? Jumper cables for feeling the promises of God are true for your whole being. They are jumper cables that really make us feel that Jesus is within us by the power of the Holy Spirit. Tony's example of the Holy Spirit is just one of the many examples of how God works in us when we give ourselves to be abandoned to Him and seek the Holy Spirit to work through us. All of this is to one end: to glorify Him and to live with Him in love, enjoying Him and glorifying Him forever.

> May the God of hope fill you with all joy and peace as you trust in him, so that you may overflow with hope by the power of the Holy Spirit.
>
> —ROMANS 15:13

FINDING FELICITY

Felicity was a servant-saint who lived around the year AD 200. She was executed because she refused to renounce her belief in God. Even when she was put in an arena with a wild bull, she did not deny Christ, but died praising Him. Hers is a story of a girl who desired God above all things.

Felicity teaches us that it is impossible to have God's ultimate joy if we do not truly believe and trust in Him. That attitude can be called felicity—God's tranquility personified. Felicity, the saint, had that presence within her. We should seek the same thing. Her faith in God and love for Him set a powerful example for us today.

When we come to God in repentance and faith, we rest in the peace that He will be Jehovah Jireh—the Great Provider of all. (See Gen. 22:14.) We have satisfaction, peace, and joy in God. This is evidence that we are in right standing with God and that we are subduing our sinful nature. Then the things of the world will be put in the proper perspective, and we will enjoy them more because we are aligned with Him.

The blessedness we receive from God is one that is filling and satisfying. The satisfactions we try to get from the world—material goods, admiration and respect from others, and sensual pleasures—in the long run leave us with the greatest emptiness. We think they will satisfy us, but they never live up to our expectations. The emptiness that follows is overwhelming and leads to the greatest despair, even when we have everything we want. When the football players in the Super Bowl win that championship ring—something they have sought their whole careers—there can be the greatest emptiness in the center of that ring if that victory is not from God. True felicity and satisfaction are not present in the world; they are present only in knowing Christ.

St. Augustine said, "Love God, and do what you want."[7] We become like God when we love Him with all of our hearts. Therefore if we love our heavenly Father, we will want to please Him. We see that St. Augustine was setting forth the basic principle of the heart. What is it that rules in our hearts? Is it love to God? God's Word tells us what love to God is like. So when we love God, we will seek to do what God's Word says. (See 1 John 5:3.) It is important that we feel God's love for us. So when we are dull of heart we need to seek Him to rekindle in our hearts that sense of His great love for us.

How does this apply to our everyday life? For years I have

been involved in the Department of Ophthalmology at the University of South Florida in Tampa. I am a clinical professor there, and I am on the board that selected the head of the department. We chose Dr. James Rowsey to come to the university from Oklahoma City.

Jim is an outstanding man. He is brilliant, pleasant, and delightful. As much as anyone I know, he exhibits the joy of God. He has also gotten into trouble. He has been sued because he prays for patients, and he has been sued by people who work for him, because they thought he was partial to other employees who are Christians.

When Jim was sued by the American Civil Liberties Union (ACLU) he realized that many of the ACLU attorneys do not believe in God. He realized that God offers His love to the attorneys of the ACLU also. He understood that the difference between them and him is that he believes and embraces God's love. One of the great lessons he learned through this difficulty was how essential it is for the one who knows God's love to pray for those who do not know that love. Jim has always had to face difficulties because of his Christian commitment, but his joy in knowing Jesus just overcomes the problems.

What has Dr. Rowsey achieved at the University of South Florida? He was able to revive a department that was dying. It came alive again; he reopened the eye center there. He has done it all on one foundation—the joy of the Lord. His joy is sincere and genuine. It comes from knowing who Christ is. This joy is meek and humble and beautiful.

It is also very effective. Dr. Rowsey influences everyone around him. He has Jewish people and people from all over the Arab world working with him, and he is able to influence them. He is a person who stands strongly for his Christian faith.

Richard Baxter, a seventeenth-century theologian, noted that love, desire, hope, and courage lead us to a joy in God.

He said these emotions, these affections or influences over the heart, flow from our innermost being as we praise God for the excellence of Christ. Then we turn away and find that external joys mean nothing without Christ in them.

We call it "enlarging the neck" because these affections basically make an opening between the head and heart. Everything we think about must be contemplated in godly ways, and those things become part of our heart and permeate our whole body. While it's important to think about these things, it is also important to have lively affections for them. We cannot only make logic within our head; we must praise with our heart.

A person's heart is the source of his or her joy. Everything must promote that joy. It is necessary for the heart to elevate the soul in what Baxter called "heavenly contemplations."[8] We must love and be loved. Then we feel this felicity, this afterglow, this all-desiring affection of being close to God.

Felicity is another way of describing the influence of the Holy Spirit in our lives. He gives the fruit of the Spirit, including joy and contentment. This felicity varies within us because we are not always totally committed to the Lord. For heaven knows that all of us have let our thoughts and our actions become sinful, and we have felt the eclipse of God's felicity and tranquility. There are times when we are so full of everything in life that is not of felicity. We are filled with the things of the world, and we are taken away from our fellowship with the Lord. Remembering the times of felicity breaks our hearts and brings us back to Him. We are restored and no longer travel the road that leads to further deceit and hurt.

So often we have wandered along and contented ourselves with vain shadows and false imaginations of piety and religion, not truly believing in His promises. The affections that lead to felicity are stirred by divine impressions and touched by our faith in Him. When you see a fellow brother or sister in Christ and they have an abundance of joy and happiness, we are seeing the Holy Spirit's overflow of joy in their life. This is the blessing we must seek with our whole heart. Let each of us pray:

Lord, help me to open my eyes and see that my whole purpose is to love You and enjoy You forever in a state of joy and contentment in the Holy Spirit.

4

TRAITS OF A
RELINQUISHED LIFE

Author C. S. Lewis described joy as a "meaningful accel-
eration, a rhythm with the character of God."[1] We don't
sit still. We physically and mentally become more and more
involved in the character of God, because we are surrendered
to Him. Let's go back to Galatians 2:20. It says, "I no longer live,
but Christ lives in me." This means we want what God wants.
We become more and more like Him.

Have you ever been around a couple who have been married a long time? Their marriage has transformed them. They
have become like each other. In fact, sometimes they finish each
other's sentences because they are of one mind and heart. There
is a harmony between them. Their love for each other fills them
with joy, peace, gentleness, and goodness. And that attitude carries over into their relationships with other people. Their loving
relationship has truly united them.

A heart that is relinquished to God is not one that is proud
of its commitment and feels self-righteous. No, it is one that
realizes, "I am nothing; Jesus is everything. I can do nothing. I
need Him for everything." A relinquished heart is a heart that
is broken and emptied of the love of self. It is filled with humble
gratitude that the Son of God would love and pity a sinner like

me and fill me with His gracious presence.

When we relinquish ourselves in faith to God, we have a divine life through our Lord and Savior. Our surrendered hearts find joy in the Lord, and our lives are filled with the same qualities as that married couple—love, joy, peace, patience, kindness, goodness, faithfulness, gentleness, and self-control. (See Gal. 5:22–23.) This fruit of the Holy Spirit changes us, and our relationships with others change as a result.

As we stand close to God, His image is stamped on us. We are transformed. It cannot be any other way. It is inevitable that we are because the Holy Spirit lives in us.

> Do not conform any longer to the pattern of this world, but be transformed by the renewing of your mind. Then you will be able to test and approve what God's will is— his good, pleasing and perfect will.
>
> —ROMANS 12:2

Our being must be transformed from the inside out. Our old thought processes must be taken captive as we are renewed by His Word and in prayer and worship—through the enablement and encouragement of the Holy Spirit. Our lives are changed through faith and surrender to God. Let's look at some of the changes that occur as we give our hearts and minds to God.

THE ETERNAL VIEW

As an ophthalmologist, I see a lot of people who are nearsighted. They only see the things that are up close. All of us can be nearsighted spiritually, seeing only the things that are up close in ourselves and in those around us. We can fail to see the overall view. James 4:14 describes this nearsightedness, "Why, you do not even know what will happen tomorrow. What is your life? You are a mist that appears for a little while and then vanishes."

That is the way we are if we don't relinquish our lives with the help of the Holy Spirit. When we are selfish and caught up in our own daily dramas, we cannot truly see. When we believe in His promises, our focus is no longer on the things of this world. We see the distant view—the eternity, the greatness of all divine reality. That is when we begin to comprehend who God really is.

Remember Psalm 73:25? "Whom have I in heaven but you? And earth has nothing I desire besides you." When our hearts are relinquished to God through the Holy Spirit, we no longer put our faith in our own abilities, but we trust in God. Isaiah 2:22 says, "Stop trusting in man, who has but a breath in his nostrils. Of what account is he?"

When we are centered on God, we have a fuller, deeper understanding of how much we need the Lord, and we are able to worship Him for His power and majesty. As we stand close to Him, the things of this world are put in proper perspective, and we can enjoy them as we align ourselves with Him.

When we truly deal with God in repentance and faith, we hand over our egos, our independence, our desires, and our worries about the future. It is not easy to give up this control. As human beings we like to be in charge of our lives. And the world tells us that we should be in control. God must humble us and crush us completely before we will seek God and see God as we ought. But when we see through God's eyes, we understand that He alone can satisfy us. He will provide for us. And we learn more and more to trust implicitly in Him.

As we struggle with this battle for control of our lives, remember these words:

> Trust in the LORD with all your heart and lean not on your own understanding; in all your ways acknowledge him, and he will make your paths straight.
> —PROVERBS 3:5–6

PEACE BEYOND COMPREHENSION

Let's look at a rubber band. It is either at ease or stretched. And if it is stretched too tightly, it can break. We frequently are like a stretched rubber band. We are at the breaking point because we are busy trying to do things by our own power. And when we are trying to be in control, basically we are caught up in the sin of selfishness. At that point we are stretched and tense like an over-extended rubber band. We are not at peace, and we do not have the joy that comes from a relationship with God. We are acting like three year olds who want to do it all by themselves. And just as parents often do, God will let us fall to teach us that we need His help.

This brings us back to the Holy Spirit's work of felicity in our hearts—God's tranquility personified. The way to find the peaceful life of a rubber band at ease is to be surrendered, relinquished, and resting in the Lord. If we rest totally in Him, we are not stretched. If we relinquish ourselves to Him to do His work, we are at ease. This comes by resting in His Word—in the promises He spoke by His mouth to our hearts. If we are busy praying and praising His majesty, we are at peace because we are where the Lord wants us to be, doing what He created us to do. We are filled with His tranquility.

Certainly we can think we have found happiness and joy while living with sin, but it is a false happiness and joy. With every activity, we are stretched tighter and tighter. Instead, we need to be at rest in God, which brings us real felicity.

Being surrendered to God can be like skiing. In skiing, when I am ready to make a turn, I lower myself and look downhill. My knees go down into the hill, my feet go down an edge, and my whole body drops. This is called anticipation. I simply look down the hill with my whole body dropping and ready. Depending on the slope is like depending on the Lord. When I depend

29

on the slope, skiing becomes easy and I expend much less effort. I can ski down the slope through the turn with ease. When that turn is done, I get ready to anticipate the next one and prepare myself for getting through it. I go from one state of anticipation to another, and the skiing is fun and easy.

How do we apply that to our daily lives? When we go through the turns in a state of anticipation with God, believing in His promises, then it is easy to ski through the smooth terrain. When we follow the pull of His gravity, we can negotiate the rough spots better, and we are filled with joy in living with Him.

We have no agenda other than resting in the Lord and listening to Him. We seek the Holy Spirit, through faith and prayer, to dominate our direction. We do not try to manipulate what happens. We ask the Holy Spirit to determine our time, our mood, and our action. We just say, "Holy Spirit, my life is Yours." I'm going to be responsive to You today."

> Do not be anxious about anything, but in everything, by prayer and petition, with thanksgiving, present your requests to God. And the peace of God, which transcends all understanding, will guard your hearts and your minds in Christ Jesus.
>
> —PHILIPPIANS 4:6–7

There is a lot of talk about burnout in today's world, especially concerning the way it affects mothers, fathers, nurses, doctors, teachers, or caregivers. But when we trust in God's faithfulness, we feel the rigorous demands of life less. By worshiping God's majesty and feeling His joy, we find God's enablement to face of all of life's challenges. We are not inactive or passive; we are active—even energetic—in our dependency on God. This dependency on Him, through our relinquishment, is the key to a joy-filled life.

One of the great spiritual lessons the famous missionary, Hudson Taylor, learned while on the mission field in China was where to rest his faith. While in England he learned to trust God for his needs without letting any other person know about them.[2] God honored this faith by providing for him. He continued the principle while in China. However, when more and more young missionaries came to the field under his care, he struggled with a need for greater faith. As he wrestled in his soul with this burden, God broke through to take him a step further. God taught him to not trust in his faith but to trust in God's faithfulness. It is in His faithfulness, not our faith, that we must put our trust. As Hudson learned to "feed on His faithfulness" (Ps. 37:3, NKJV), his burden was lifted and his joy returned. God's faithfulness that we rest in is our source of peace and joy in the midst of all our trials. Let us listen to what the Spirit of God says: "He who calls you is faithful, who also will do it" (1 Thess. 5:24, NKJV). "He who promised is faithful" (Heb. 10:23, NKJV).

There are times when all of us feel that the burden of the cares of life is too heavy for us to bear. There are things about our lives that we cannot control. There is one answer to our dilemma, and that is to rest in and rejoice in God's faithfulness. The peace and joy that we find when we trust in Him are a sure pledge that His joy will be perfected and continue to fill us through all eternity. I invite you to pray with me:

Dear Lord, help me to rest in You. Take my burdens and let me enjoy the peace that comes with surrendering my life to You. Lord, let your Holy Spirit fill every inch of me. Direct me! Convict me! Give me wisdom and strength!

OBEDIENCE

The apostle Paul, writing to the Philippians, describes Jesus as our role model since He is the perfect example of this surrender:

> Your attitude should be the same as that of Christ Jesus: Who, being in very nature God, did not consider equality with God something to be grasped, but made himself nothing, taking the very nature of a servant, being made in human likeness. And being found in appearance as a man, he humbled himself and became obedient to death—even death on a cross!
>
> —*PHILIPPIANS 2:5–8*

So to live as Christ did, we must be humble, obedient, and ready to die to our own selfishness. That sounds like a difficult assignment. But this is not some dreary task that is placed upon us as Christians. When we desire God above all other things, we are excited to love Him, believe in Him, obey Him, and serve Him. We experience the trust that comes from faith in His grace. As the apostle Paul explained: "The life I live in the body, I live by faith in the Son of God, who loved me and gave himself for me" (Gal. 2:20).

Consider the rewards of this joyous mind-set. We have the assurance that God is in control of our lives. And we receive the benefits of following a God who loves us and will provide for us.

> The LORD is my light and my salvation—whom shall I fear? The LORD is the stronghold of my life—of whom shall I be afraid?
>
> —*PSALM 27:1*

We must never think of our relinquishment to God as arising from our own initiative, determination, or merit before God. Those attitudes reflect pride. We were all like sheep going astray when Jesus came and found us and laid us on His shoulders, rejoicing that He found His lost sheep. (See Luke 15:5.) We were following wrong voices and influences until He came and called us away from our self-destructive paths. Jesus said, "My sheep hear My voice, and I know them, and they follow Me" (John 10:27, NKJV).

When we are relinquished to God, we are not full of pride or arrogance or selfishness. Remember the fruit of the Spirit—love, joy, peace, patience, kindness, goodness, faithfulness, gentleness, and self-control? (See Gal. 5:22–23.) These are the qualities that fill us as we surrender ourselves to God and His will. These affect not only our relationship with God but also our relationships with others. Just like that married couple whose love spilled over into all areas of their lives, so the divine fruit of a relinquished life changes how we relate to others.

When we are relinquished to God, it is easier to give up the pretenses, pride, and self-righteousness that can destroy relationships with others. Instead, we respect others with godly dignity. And we do not need to cover things up.

The first couple, Adam and Eve, felt no need to hide anything from God or each other while they were relinquished to Him and living without sin. They were open to one another. They didn't hide their feelings. It was a truly intimate relationship. Only when they sinned did they feel the need to cover themselves with clothes and with selfish attitudes.

In the same way, we are truly intimate with others only when we are relinquished to God and feel no need to cover up or hide behind false actions and attitudes.

As you pray these prayers at the end of each chapter, remember they are your person-to-Person dealing with God in response to what He is teaching you (and me):

Father, thank You for love, joy, peace, patience, kindness, goodness, faithfulness, gentleness, and self-control. Help me to experience this fruit in my life every day. Father, You have given me Your Holy Spirit and made me Your child. You always amaze me!

5

THE STRUGGLE TO
STAY RELINQUISHED

A life of infinite, glorious joy is a life that is relinquished in faith to God. Consider the analogy of the trapeze artist who must let go of one bar before he can start swinging on the next one. In that same way, we must relinquish the bar of the world so we can grab the bar of the Lord. We must learn more and more to desire the things of this world no longer, but to turn everything over to Him.

And just as a trapeze artist swings from bar to bar, so we struggle with totally relinquishing ourselves to God. It is not a one-time event. It is a process as we build our relationship with God the Father, God the Son, and God the Holy Spirit. It is like your relationship with your spouse. That relationship did not happen overnight. There was the time you first met, the time you realized you were in love, and the time you truly committed yourself to that person. And even after that commitment, the two of you did not have perfect unity all the time. You have had disagreements and misunderstandings as you have learned to live together. But when harmony and unity are restored, the love is greater; the joy at being back together and still being in love is sweeter. And you have gained a deeper understanding of your spouse.

BELIEVE AND REJOICE

We are that way with God. We love Him, we commit ourselves to Him, but we still struggle in the relationship. We find it difficult to give up our independence; and sometimes we still think there might be something better out there than what He can provide. Too often we draw back from surrendering ourselves fully to God.

A LESSON IN TRUST

The Scriptures are filled with examples of people's struggles to stay surrendered to God.

One example in the Old Testament is King Asa. When Asa started his reign, he was a great warrior and religious reformer. He trusted God for great things and had found God to be faithful in doing things beyond what Asa could ask or think.

"LORD, there is no one like you to help the powerless against the mighty. Help us, O LORD our God, for we rely on you, and in your name we have come against this vast army. O LORD, you are our God; do not let man prevail against you," Asa prayed in 2 Chronicles 14:11. And Asa and his troops were victorious in battle.

But then Asa's kingdom was threatened by the king in the north of Israel, Baasha. Rather than trusting God, Asa cut a deal with the king of Syria for help. He forgot that with God nothing shall be impossible. The prophet Hanani rebuked Asa for relying on Syria rather than on the Lord. The king was so angry he put the prophet in chains and continued to turn away from God. What did Hanani tell him?

> For the eyes of the LORD range throughout the earth to strengthen those whose hearts are fully committed to him.
>
> —2 CHRONICLES 16:9

The king forgot how God provided for him and turned from his trust in God. He turned to others rather than trusting God. Hanani called him to remember God's love and power.

Asa forgot that God delights to show Himself strong on behalf of those whose hearts are set on Him. The verse says "whose hearts are fully committed to him." Other translations say "those whose heart is perfect toward him" or "blameless toward Him." The Hebrew word translated "committed" is from the root verb, *shalom*, which means "completing a vow or fulfilling a covenant" (Strong's #7999). It is used again when Nehemiah rebuilt the walls of Jerusalem. He *shalomed* the walls, meaning he completed them (see Neh. 6:15, NKJV). Those whose hearts are shalomed toward God are "completed" or "blameless" toward Him. They are at peace—shalom—with God.

Let's look at a modern story about someone who had that true shalom. Aniefiok Udo was the son of a Nigerian tribal chief who was killed during the civil war there in the late 1960s. The war set tribe against tribe, group against group, and many people were killed. At this time, Aniefiok was in his early teens. He was so angry and resentful because of his father's death that he was "always fighting with knives on the pretext that [he] wanted to kill someone."[1] However, his anger and resentment almost killed *him*.

Whether his grave condition was caused by physical, mental, or psychological factors is unknown, but he was near death. He recognized that his hatred and despair were a big part of his illness. Then he met the Lord. Aniefiok was changed from a man of hatred and despair to a man of joy, with a smile that extended from ear to ear. He talked about God confirming His call in his life—to serve Him wherever He would send him.

Aniefiok has earned five college degrees, graduating from Dallas Theological Seminary, always at the top of his class. He has done well because he changed from a man who totally depended on his anger to handle life situations to one who totally rests in the Lord, surrendering himself and believing in God's eternal promises. The fulfilling of God within his heart has given him peace and joy.

Those whose hearts are perfect toward God are those whose hearts are shalomed toward Him. When we trust not in our own strength, but fix our sights on God's majesty, we have joyous, relinquished hearts that trust and depend on Him and believe in His promises.

My God and my King, may my heart never forget Your promises, and may I be transformed through surrender to You.

LESSONS IN DAILY LIFE

Just as King Asa was drawn away from a relationship with God, we face temptations today. Often we find ourselves lured by the things and ways of this world. We get diverted in our walk with God, and we lose our joy in Him. Our focus shifts from God to ourselves, and we try to take back what we once relinquished to Him.

Why does this happen? Sometimes things are going well in our lives and we begin to depend on these happy circumstances. Then we forget to trust in Him and begin to think that we can actually take the credit for the good in our lives.

Or sometimes we get caught up in our troubles. We get so focused on them that they pull us down deeper and deeper, and we forget to seek God. A truly relinquished heart feels true joy in God's presence. But there are times when we feel God is far away. Proverbs 13:12 says, "Hope deferred makes the heart sick, but a longing fulfilled is a tree of life." All of us have had goals or hopes for our lives fall through. But our hearts get sick when we get wrapped up in the disappointment and grief. Then we begin down a path of bitterness, resentment, and self-pity that feeds on our selfishness. We did not get what we wanted, and we sulk about it.

There is no room for God in that mind-set. We are not relinquished. We are selfish and want to wallow in our misery. Then the Spirit of God moves within us. We realize the distance between our hearts and Him. We are lonely and frustrated. We see that we cannot rely on ourselves. Then we turn back to God, who is our portion and our all in all. And the joy of reuniting with His presence fills us. As the psalmist wrote:

> You turned my wailing into dancing; you removed my sackcloth and clothed me with joy.
>
> —PSALM 30:11

Dear Lord, help me every day to examine myself and relinquish every area of my life to You. For in Your loving arms I am filled, not with the delights of this world, but with Your joy.

DOING OR BEING?

I have to admit to something. Every day, I am one of the first people to get up, get organized, and start moving vigorously, churning from one task to another. If I am not careful, all this energy that goes to completing tasks distracts me from relying on the Lord to fill me with His presence.

I have to remember that everything I do in my tasks and errands and duties is short-lived. The eternal things are unseen. As I focus on them by faith, I have the pleasures of God in my heart and the love of God in my works.

The Gospel of Luke tells a story about two sisters with a similar conflict between actions of the hands and attitudes of the heart.

Jesus and His disciples stopped at the home of Mary and Martha to visit and eat. Martha scurried around getting things ready for the meal, and she became agitated because Mary just sat at Jesus' feet, listening to what He said. Martha asked Him, "Lord, don't you care that my sister has left me to do the work by myself? Tell her to help me!" (Luke 10:40). And Jesus replied:

> "Martha, Martha," the Lord answered, "you are worried and upset about many things, but only one thing is needed. Mary has chosen what is better, and it will not be taken away from her."
>
> —LUKE 10:41–42

There are a lot of us out there who are like Martha. We are geared toward getting things done, checking them off "to do" lists, and moving on to some other task. My secretary (who happens to be a preacher's wife) and I are the same way; we are both Marthas. And every morning, Lois and I look at each other and smile. And I say, "Lois, you and I are going to be Marys today." She says, "OK." And she smiles because we are both such Marthas.

But those of us who are Marthas are not hopeless, as long as we remember what is most important: we must surrender ourselves daily in faith to God.

Every year, our family goes skiing during Christmas vacation. I used to read the Bible through during that short vacation. That is being a Martha. But if I remember to look into the Lord's eyes as I read, I could become a Mary. I have to ask, *Did I really look for Christ in my reading or was I too busy getting the job done—just reading the Bible through? Was I asking the Lord to fill me with His presence as I read, or was I too intent on my goal?* We are either asking Him to reveal His life within us, or we have diverted our gaze from Him.

The first thing I do in the mornings when I get up is bless

my wife. She asks me, "Are you being a Mary or Martha in this blessing?" When I read my Bible during Christmas vacation, she asks, "Are you being a Mary or a Martha?" Heather helps me remember to stop and listen to God, to work out a closeness with Him that helps me to relinquish myself daily to Him.

I invite you to pray with me:

> *Lord, teach me as a Martha to become more like Mary. Teach me to not try to prove myself by tasks and deeds, however good they might be. Teach me to come close to You in meekness. Teach me to be open and honest and show me that nothing matters other than You.*

WHAT WE WANT, OR WHAT GOD WANTS?

A heart at peace gives life to the body, but envy rots the bones.

—PROVERBS 14:30

Coveting may be one of the biggest things that keeps us from having a relinquished spirit. The dictionary says that coveting is to long for with envy. For Christians, it means that our hearts desire something other than Jesus.

In envy, the Pharisees delivered Christ to be crucified. Good came out of it because Christ was in it. But frequently that envy, or covetousness, is the epitome of sins that separate us from the ability to be relinquished. And if we are not relinquished, we do not have true joy.

In all facets of life we can destroy ourselves by wanting the wrong things or even too much of what we already have. We want when we need not. Our wants keep us from having the joy of relationships that are godly—a godly relationship with each other and a godly relationship with our Redeemer.

People who want a lot of things are frequently anxious about everything and sensitive to everything—their personal lives, their work, and their relationships. Some people even destroy their marriages by wanting other things, especially if they become involved in other relationships. Mark 4:19 says, "But the worries of this life, the deceitfulness of wealth and the desires for other things come in and choke the word, making it unfruitful."

I see this inner, destructive motive in my own attitudes; I see it in my relationships with colleagues; I see it in interpersonal relationships. It destroys our productivity, our peace within our work, and everything else in our lives, because we are envious of someone else. Instead of being thankful for what we have and feeling grateful and blessed, we feel envious to the point of negating our own place in life and, certainly, our communion with Christ. Envy of worldly things takes away from our surrender to Him, because it prevents us from being relinquished. It keeps us in the world rather than focused on the eternal. It keeps us from expressing faith and joy.

The things we want also keep us from enjoying the things we have. There is an old story about four cows in a field. The field was fenced off into four sections and each cow had her own section to enjoy. Yet each cow had her neck through the fence, trying to get the grass in another cow's section.

Coveting gives us more anxiety and less pleasure. The relinquished life doesn't mean we have "things." When we believe God's promises we are filled with joy, peace, and righteousness. An abandoned faith puts God first, and then we are able to more fully enjoy what He has given us.

The best example is a story Jesus told in Luke 16:19–26:

There was a rich man who was dressed in purple and fine linen and lived in luxury every day. At his gate was laid a beggar named Lazarus, covered with sores and longing to eat what fell from the rich man's table. Even the dogs came and licked his sores.

The time came when the beggar died and the angels carried him to Abraham's side. The rich man also died and was buried. In hell, where he was in torment, he looked up and saw Abraham far away, with Lazarus by his side. So he called to him, "Father Abraham, have pity on me and send Lazarus to dip the tip of his finger in water and cool my tongue, because I am in agony in this fire."

But Abraham replied, "Son, remember that in your lifetime you received your good things, while Lazarus received bad things, but now he is comforted here and you are in agony. And besides all this, between us and you a great chasm has been fixed, so that those who want to go from here to you cannot, nor can anyone cross over from there to us."

Jesus tells us that there is no correlation between what we have on Earth and what we have when we die. Even though Lazarus had nothing and was physically in shame on Earth, he had turned his life over to God. And while the rich man had everything, he was proud and arrogant. It kept him from being relinquished. And their positions were reversed when they died. Lazarus is at the right side of Abraham, and the rich man is in torment in hell.

Does this mean that if we have worldly goods we will spend eternity in hell? Not at all. Our possessions do not matter to God. Our attitude toward them does. What we need is abandoned faith and a relinquished spirit. Lazarus had nothing to prevent him from being relinquished; the rich man did. Sometimes we let our possessions or desires keep us from turning to

43

God. Then we struggle with surrendering those things to Him.

We must remember to keep our attitude toward earthly possessions in check. If we begin to believe our possessions make us important, we put our trust in them and become proud and arrogant, depending on our own abilities. But if we remember that everything comes from God, we can keep our focus on Him and live a life that is relinquished to His will. A mighty king of Babylon, Nebuchadnezzar, learned this, and his words still speak to us today.

> Now I, Nebuchadnezzar, praise and exalt and glorify the King of heaven, because everything he does is right and all his ways are just. And those who walk in pride he is able to humble.
>
> —DANIEL 4:37

Dear God, may my eyes never lose sight of You, that I can focus on eternal treasures and not the possessions of this world. Show me my pride daily so it does not hinder me from walking with You!

THE WORRY DISEASE

I would love to be in the stock market. I did some trading when I was young, but it made me worry about what was happening in the world. I was constantly concerned about all the dynamics of the world—the politics, the monetary system, the business cycles, and the ever-intruding Marxist philosophy in various economics.

So I distanced myself, refusing to allow myself to worry. I found that when I would come back to even thinking about it in a very cursory way, just by reading a lot about business and getting involved in planning projects, I removed myself from the peace that I normally had, and I found myself worrying again.

And that mentality was certainly not as peaceful or desirable or joyful as the philosophy of simply loving and caring for people in my medical practice.

The lesson I learned was that I had to be relinquished to God. I had to give up worrying about the future and trying to control what would happen to me. I had to forget the worries of the world and believe in God's eternal promises. For us to truly relinquish ourselves to God we have to quit thinking in earthly terms and trust in His agenda and timetable.

> Therefore we do not lose heart. Though outwardly we are wasting away, yet inwardly we are being renewed day by day. For our light and momentary troubles are achieving for us an eternal glory that far outweighs them all. So we fix our eyes not on what is seen, but on what is unseen. For what is seen is temporary, but what is unseen is eternal.
> —2 CORINTHIANS 4:16–18

In the medical profession, we see patients who frequently worry themselves sick. They create problems so they have something to worry about. And worry becomes the worst disease I see. It destroys people by destroying the quality of their life, the length of their life—every part of their life. People do this not only with their bodies, but in all facets of their lives. Anticipation is always worse than the dreaded deed.

In sporting activities some people worry so much that they destroy their ability to perform at their best. For example, one of the most important things golfers can do is relax and concentrate. But they can worry so much that it affects their game. That is true in any sport. It is very important that we are aware of our elapsed time when running or our golf score when we are on the course. But we cannot be overcome and let those things make us worry. If we worry too much, we are beaten in a mind game.

We can destroy relationships in the same way. Sometimes two people want to become very close, yet one person is always worrying. That worrying prevents real intimacy because the other person can get only so close without getting caught up in that unhealthy worry mentality. Many husbands and wives have a problem with a spouse who worries too much. It is difficult to have a healthy mental attitude and still be close to such a spouse.

What do we do if we have a spouse whose worrying transcends every part of his or her life? Love them, care for them, pray for them, and wait for them to get through that stage so they can blossom. You want them to not worry, so you have to relinquish them to the Lord. By relinquishing them, you also give yourself to the Lord, so you do not get pulled down into that whirlpool of worry. You must be close to your mate, but you must be relinquished at the same time. Anything less and we self-destruct. We must abandon ourselves to God's promises, like John Wesley did at Aldersgate. Worry is the devil's stronghold in us. Trust in God's grace is what sustains us.

My colleague, Gary Carter, has wisely analyzed the sin of worry:

- What are we really saying when we worry?

We are saying:

- Maybe God doesn't care.

- Maybe God isn't good.

- Maybe God's promises aren't true.

- Maybe God isn't in control.

- Maybe God isn't sovereign.

- Maybe God doesn't work all things for good for those who love Him.

- Maybe God isn't all-wise in the trials He sends us.

- Maybe God isn't a faithful Father.

- What terrible things to say! Let us think about what we are really saying when we worry.

It seems we fall prey to the things we worry about the most. I refuse to worry in my medical practice. I will continue to relinquish myself to the Lord so I can practice the best medicine possible and delight myself in His presence as I try to take care of people.

If I worried about all the facets of my life, life would become just what I worried about. If throughout the day I relinquish myself to Him, to His joy, and to His glorious countenance, I become like Him.

We have the choice to enjoy life or to destroy it with worry and want. When we worry too much, we show that we do not trust the Lord. And when we try to be happy externally and artificially, it fades quickly. We must refuse to worry and want; we have to care only to be relinquished to Him in love. There are many characteristics necessary for any activity—quickness as a tennis player, strength as a football player, and submission to the will of God as a Christian. Through submission we will enjoy God's favor.

There is only one answer—relinquishing ourselves to God in absolute faith in His grace. Such a faith declares that He is our answer to everything. The power of the Resurrection is the answer to all. How often we need to pray this prayer:

Dear Lord, keep me strong in my faith in You and Your grace. Help me to put my faith in You when I am more inclined to trust in myself. Help me to not be distracted by the trials of daily life, but instead, to rely on Your

*love and strength. Keep me focused on the big picture of
who You are and what You are going to do for me!*

A CRITICAL SPIRIT

Love is essential for us to truly relinquish our lives in faith to
God. But sometimes our pride gets the better of us. We can
develop a habit of criticizing others to build up ourselves, and we
lose sight of that love. We become accusers rather than interces-
sors. And when that happens, we end up destroying ourselves
and the things that are most important to us.

A similar thing happened to Jacob in the Old Testament.
Jacob tricked his father, Isaac, into giving him the blessing that
rightfully belonged to his older brother, Esau. Then his mother
sent him to live with her brother, Laban. While there, Jacob
fell in love with Laban's daughter, Rachel. He made a deal with
Laban. He would work for him for seven years in exchange for
Rachel's hand in marriage.

But on the wedding day, Laban tricked Jacob, giving him
Rachel's older sister, Leah. So then Jacob had to work another
seven years to marry his true love, Rachel.

These two deceitful men lived on the same land until it
became unbearable. One night, Jacob gathered up his family
and possessions, including all the herds he owned, and left without telling Laban. While the family was packing, Rachel stole
her father's household gods, without telling Jacob. Laban was
angry that Jacob left and that the household gods were missing,
so he chased Jacob.

When Laban found him, he confronted Jacob about the
missing gods. He accused Jacob of taking not only his daughters,
but his herds and, of course, the household gods. Laban's pride
and anger needed to try and put Jacob down one last time.

Jacob defended himself, saying the women and herds were

rightfully his. He had worked hard for them. Then he said he did not know anything about the missing gods, and he told Laban to look around. He also issued this curse, which would come back to haunt him, "But if you find anyone who has your gods, he shall not live" (Gen. 31:32).

Now, Jacob did not know that Rachel had hidden her father's possessions in her saddlebag. Without knowing it, he cursed the only thing he truly cared for—his wife Rachel. Laban did not find the missing gods, and he and Jacob parted on bitter terms. What happened to Rachel, whom Jacob unknowingly cursed? She later died in childbirth.

Now, Jacob could have told Laban, "Let me look with you and help you find them." Then the partnership would have grown and there would have been seeds of unity, not disharmony. But he did not, and he lost the one thing he loved most, his wife Rachel.

The lesson for us is to remember to keep a loving and humble spirit. We should use the art of humble questioning rather than being proud and getting critical and angry. Otherwise, we will destroy ourselves and those around us, particularly those who are closest to us.

> *Lord, help me to follow Your example of love and humility. Keep me from being critical for the sake of my own ego, and help me to act with kindness, not pride.*

6

RELINQUISHED OR RELIGIOUS?

Surrender...submission...selflessness. When we submit ourselves to God, we find ourselves filled with joy. When we relinquish our egos and independence to God, we find ourselves filled with glorious, abundant joy. We are at peace with ourselves because we have found peace in God. Then we are full of joy because we love God and depend on Him—not ourselves. However, let us never forget that it is receiving the love of God by believing His promises that is the fountain of our inner life toward God. Jesus said:

> Whoever drinks of the water that I shall give him will never thirst. But the water that I shall give him will become in him a fountain of water springing up into everlasting life.
>
> —JOHN 4:14, NKJV

Earlier we talked about how the temptations and problems of the world can lure us away from a relinquished life. But some of our fiercest struggles can be as followers of Christ—when we get so busy "doing" all the right things that we forget to be still and listen to Christ and follow Him. We do not have peace and joy because we are too busy doing things.

Within all of us there is a tug between the relinquished

spirit and a religious one. Now, on the surface, having a religious spirit sounds like a good thing. But by "religious spirit" I mean we are following the religious culture, going through the motions of having faith in God, but not really committing to Him; we do not love Him and we do not truly believe in His promises. We must not just appear externally as if we were religious, by calling ourselves such or belonging to an organization. A relinquished heart allows God to change us from an attitude of uncaring indifference to a life of joy and love that emanates from our hearts and is visible in our actions.

The religious spirit puts man first; the relinquished spirit focuses on God. The relinquished heart finds true joy in God. Joy is missing in a religious spirit. This is a clear concept, but our human nature makes it difficult to accomplish every day.

SUPERFICIAL SIGNS

The Old Testament gives us many examples that illustrate the problems with a religious spirit. Chapter four of 1 Samuel tells us about a series of battles between the Israelites and the Philistines. In one battle, the Israelites lost four thousand men. So they sent the message back to the city of Shiloh: bring the ark of the covenant to the battlefield. The Israelites planned to carry it into the next battle, hoping God would bless them because the ark was present.

The ark contained the tables of the law. But it also had an atonement cover (or mercy seat) to proclaim that there is forgiveness with God. The presence of that cover made it a type of God's throne representing grace. So the ark was not just a physical presence; it was a symbol of God's covenant with His people and their commitment to Him.

There was a precedent for carrying this holy symbol of God into battle. God told Joshua at the battle of Jericho to have priests march at the front of his army carrying the ark. The walls of Jericho collapsed, and Joshua's army was victorious.

But when the Israelites decided to use the ark in their battle against the Philistines, they were not following God's command; they were just looking for an edge in the fight. They wanted the outward blessing of battle—victory—without an inward devotion to God. Bringing the ark to the battle was an outward and showy attempt to manipulate God. This was the religious spirit at its worst—a spirit that relies on false actions, not heartfelt faith. It is not that what they did was just wrong. They did it with the wrong motives.

The Israelites must have been surprised at the outcome. Not only did they lose the battle, but also thirty thousand men were killed and the ark was captured by the Philistines. The whole experience was summarized in the word *ichabod*, which means "the glory has departed," or "the Lord has departed" from Shiloh and all of Israel, with the capture of the ark (Strong's # 350).

We need to examine our own lives. Do we have God before us or our own goals? Here is one way to look at it:

> I have set the LORD always before me. Because he is at my right hand, I will not be shaken.
>
> —PSALM 16:8

> *Dear God, let me not be shaken, but have my eyes fixed firmly on You. Let my actions speak for my beliefs and let me not have false attitudes and activities that do not reflect Your joy.*

SELFISH SPIRIT

When we have a religious spirit, we are focused more on ourselves and what God can do for us than we are on His majesty and grace and what we are called to do for Him. We start presenting Him with lists of demands, and we do not want to give our lives to Him as faithful servants. We are selfish and self-centered. We want to do only what is convenient for us. Jesus warns us about this attitude when He quotes the words of the prophet Isaiah as He lectures the Pharisees:

> These people honor me with their lips, but their hearts are far from me. They worship me in vain; their teachings are but rules taught by men.
> —MATTHEW 15:8–9

When we are filled with a religious spirit, our human desire to be independent takes over. We start thinking that we know best. We start relying on our own puny skills and abilities rather than on the limitless power of the almighty God.

Dr. Martyn Lloyd-Jones, who was born in 1899 in Wales, gave a speech early in his life titled "The Problem with Wales."[1] One of the problems he singled out was the use of mirrors:

> When I grew up in Wales, we didn't have many mirrors. Now, people spend so much time looking in mirrors, it gives them a conscious focus on self. They are looking at their own face and it is firmly fixed in their mind. They are all the time thinking about their appearance and the impression they make.

Our hearts are not in the right place. We may go through the motions of believing, or follow all the rules, but that does not get us anywhere. Rather than being focused on ourselves we need to follow the advice of the psalmist:

> Look to the LORD and his strength; seek his face always.
> —PSALM 105:4

Father, I mean to trust in You and let You have control of my life. But often I fail. May my joy in You keep me strong.

Pride

Humility isn't something that comes naturally to a lot of people. We want to be proud of who we are, what we accomplish, and what we own. There is a kind of true pride, but there is also the false pride of a religious spirit. Here is a warning about false pride:

> Do not keep talking so proudly or let your mouth speak such arrogance, for the LORD is a God who knows, and by him deeds are weighed.
>
> —1 SAMUEL 2:3

A relinquished heart requires purity and separation from our base human attitudes, which are constantly within us regardless of how close we are to the Lord. We frequently think we have the answer. In fact, in our own egotism we think we are "the answer" and frequently do not turn to Christ.

True humility results from submitting our lives to God and worshiping Him. We are not humble by nature. Humility is not something we can decide to acquire. We become humble only as we love and follow Him. And our submission to Him becomes all-consuming—affecting every part of our body, permeating us, and directing us. Humility is reflected in our lives when we are molded by the Holy Spirit.

> All of you, clothe yourselves with humility toward one another, because, "God opposes the proud but gives grace to the humble." Humble yourselves, therefore, under God's mighty hand, that he may lift you up in due time.
>
> —1 PETER 5:5–6

Dear God, keep my arrogance in check and remind me who You are, how much You love me, and how You will continually provide for me.

LEGALISM

When we are filled with a religious spirit, we lose our focus on God and focus rather on following man-made rules and regulations, which is easier than trying to seek God and follow His will. We quit trusting in Him, and we start trying to control our own lives.

Only the Holy Spirit can work in us to break this religious mind-set. When we focus on rules and regulations, we no longer follow God's greatest commandment: "Love the LORD your God with all your heart and with all your soul and with all your strength" (Deut. 6:5). Instead, we are filled with a spirit of legalism. The apostle Paul challenged this legalistic mind-set:

> Since you died with Christ to the basic principles of this world, why, as though you still belonged to it, do you submit to its rules: "Do not handle! Do not taste! Do not touch!"? These are all destined to perish with use, because they are based on human commands and teachings.
>
> —COLOSSIANS 2:20–22

Paul warns us how wrong this love of rules and regulations can be:

> He has made us competent as ministers of a new covenant—not of the letter [or law] but of the Spirit; for the letter kills, but the Spirit gives life.
>
> —2 CORINTHIANS 3:6

Believe and Rejoice

Jesus battled those with a spirit of legalism during His ministry here on Earth. He criticized them for following minor rules rather than focusing on loving God.

> Woe to you, teachers of the law and Pharisees, you hypocrites! You give a tenth [as your tithe]...But you have neglected the more important matters of the law—justice, mercy and faithfulness. You should have practiced the latter, without neglecting the former.
>
> —MATTHEW 23:23

This religious spirit with its dominating rules kept the Jewish leaders from being surrendered to God. They failed to adore and praise God. Jesus preached the necessity of a relinquished heart that truly surrenders to the love of God, as the psalmist wrote:

> As the deer pants for streams of water, so my soul pants for you, O God. My soul thirsts for God, for the living God. When can I go and meet with God?
>
> —PSALM 42:1–2

Jesus, remind me that You must be my focus. Let me dwell in You and be Your child for eternity.

Rebellion and Growth

C. S. Lewis would often ask intellectuals to imagine, if they could, a God who would provide for them, love them, and be their constant source of strength. Then he would philosophize with them on whether that was a good thing or a bad thing. Though it seems good, to most thinking people, we sometimes have a hard time rationalizing God.

While it is a good thing to think we were created by a Person, Elohim the Creator, and to assume that He had a design for us because He loves us, our independence and rebellion keep us from accepting that reality. To accept the fact of a loving Creator requires that we determine how He wants to relate to us and us to Him.

When we are self-centered, we do not want any other "Being," no matter how noble or legitimate their claims, to interfere with our lives. We refuse to look at life from eternity's perspective; in that sense all of our lives are lived in rebellion against God.

There is another way of looking at it. Each of us develops, to a greater or lesser extent, a passive-aggressive personality as we grow up. It can be defined like this: when your parents told you to sit down, you sat down, but you were still "standing up" on the inside. That is a form of rebellion. Now, as we mature, we may relinquish that rebellion for love of God and others. Then we learn to serve one another and submit to one another.

Otherwise, that rebellion in us can evolve into defiance, which makes us selfish. We insist on always having our own way and are difficult to live with. We can become manipulative, destructive, frustrated, unhappy, and angry.

We develop similarly in our relationship with God as we struggle to give up our pride and independence and be relinquished to Him. We learn to live in His presence. And that helps us destroy our mental, physical, and sinful rebellion, and we become one with Him.

If we do not mature and learn to submit to Him and serve Him in love, God will have to chasten and rebuke us, for He is determined to teach all of His children how to walk humbly with their God. (See Mic. 6:8.) An Old Testament story helps us remember this: a man named Nabal, a wealthy man who is described as surly and mean, rejected David's request for some provisions for himself and his men. Not only did he reject the request, but he abused and insulted David. And David, being human, was angered. He told his men to get ready for battle because he intended to destroy Nabal and everything that belonged to him.

Nabal's wife, Abigail, caught wind of what was happening. Without wasting any time, she went to David, bringing an abundance of food and wine, so she could calm him down and save her husband. When she got to David, she asked for his forgiveness, and told him that he would find great satisfaction if wisdom and grace replaced his anger. She spoke with assurance that God would keep him safe, and he need not be troubled by people such as her husband:

> Yet a man has risen to pursue you and seek your life, but the life of my lord shall be bound in the bundle of the living with the LORD your God; and the lives of your enemies He shall sling out, as from the pocket of a sling.
>
> —1 SAMUEL 25:29, NKJV

Abigail reminded David that the Lord was his reason for living (his life was bound up in the bundle of life with the Lord) and to put aside his anger. This helped David calm down and gave him a greater perspective. David remembered that he had to surrender to God and submit to His control.

We must mature in our relationship with God. Central to all our growth in God is to realize that Jesus must be our portion in this life—our greatest joy—and that the joy of the Lord is our strength.

The following prayer is not one we can pray just once or twice; we need to pray daily:

> *Heavenly Father, even though I am Your child, I do not want to be childish. Help me grow and mature in my love, and help me surrender continually to You.*

7

RESTORED TO JOY

It is a daily struggle to stay relinquished to God. Sometimes we fail. Our desire for independence and control takes over; we forget God's promises, and we turn away from Him. And our lives can become consumed with bitterness, hatred, frustration, and anger. We are living in sin because we are not living in God's presence.

But God gives us a path back to Him, a way to restore the relationship. When we confess our sin and repent, we experience overwhelming joy in renewing our communion with Him again.

> Create in me a pure heart, O God, and renew a steadfast spirit within me. Do not cast me from your presence or take your Holy Spirit from me. Restore to me the joy of your salvation and grant me a willing spirit, to sustain me.
> —PSALM 51:10–12

In this psalm, David writes of the joy of coming back into a right relationship with God. When we confess our sin and repent, we experience overwhelming joy in knowing Him again. We are filled with wonder and awe at His grace and worship His greatness and majesty. Separation from God means sadness. Reunion with Him means joy and gladness.

Confessing our sin is an important step on the path of a relinquished heart. When we confess, we admit that we have sinned against God's love. Jesus tells a story in Luke 15 to illustrate this. A son asked his father for his inheritance, took the money, and traveled far from home. He squandered all the money, and then he was forced to look for work.

He could only find one job—feeding pigs. He realized his working conditions were worse than those of his father's workers. He decided to go home and ask his father to treat him as he would any other hired hand. "The son said to him, 'Father, I have sinned against heaven and against you. I am no longer worthy to be called your son'" (Luke 15:21).

But the father was not angry that his son had wasted his money and time. He did not take him back as an employee and say, "I told you so," or lecture him. Instead, he rejoiced that his son had come home. He said, "Bring the fattened calf and kill it. Let's have a feast and celebrate. For this son of mine was dead and is alive again; he was lost and is found" (Luke 15:23–24).

Too often we are like that son. We rely on our own abilities and skills, and we do not trust in the Lord with all our hearts. We are ungrateful when we receive blessings from God, and we do not give Him the credit. And we do not admit that we are living in this sinful attitude. Our actions speak louder than our false words. They show that we do not believe God is worthy of our loyalty. We have turned from a relinquished spirit to a false pride and trust in our own strength and understanding.

As the prodigal son confessed his unworthiness, so we must admit that we have dishonored God. We do not confess because we were caught at our sin or were embarrassed by it. We must confess because we have offended the God who loves us. As Proverbs 28:13 says, "He who conceals his sins does not prosper, but whoever confesses and renounces them finds mercy." We must be honest, we must be specific, and we must be thorough when we confess our sins to God.

Father, I am such a rebellious child. Lord, my motives were from love of myself, not love and praise of You.

SEEKING GOD'S FORGIVENESS

After we have confessed our sins, we must ask God's forgiveness: "Oh, pity and forgive me by the blood of Christ." When we ask His forgiveness, we surrender ourselves to Him and are cleansed. Then nothing stands between our Redeemer and us.

Then we must rise up and praise Him for forgiveness. We believe it. We embrace it. We delight in it. "I'm forgiven! I'm clean before the Lord!" After all, God has promised He would forgive us. It is His desire for us to ask. First John 1:9 says, "If we confess our sins, he is faithful and just and will forgive us our sins and purify us from all unrighteousness." Second Chronicles 7:14 says, "If my people, who are called by my name, will humble themselves and pray and seek my face and turn from their wicked ways, then will I hear from heaven and will forgive their sin and will heal their land." We treat God as a liar if we do not truly believe we are forgiven and rejoice.

Then we have the joy of being free from the guilt of sin. Until we seek His forgiveness, we cannot have that kind of joy. That forgiveness, that freedom is essential.

Because we are human, we all seem to wander right back into things that we should not do; we deviate from His standard. So asking forgiveness is not just a one-time event. We need to constantly be aware of our thoughts, our actions, our lack of action, and anything else in which we fail. Paul describes this state of sinful living in Romans 14:23, "Everything that does not come from faith is sin." Let us not be of anything other than faith in Him. We should have no agenda other than seeking to please Him, to fellowship with Him, to serve Him, and to seek forgiveness when we sin.

Dear Lord, forgive me when I stray from You and lose sight of Your glory, majesty, and love. I praise You for Your mercy, grace, and forgiveness, which frees me from the bondage of sin.

REPENTANCE

If you repent, I will restore you.

—JEREMIAH 15:19

Repentance is bittersweet. The sweetness comes from God's forgiveness, welcome, and acceptance of us because of Jesus' death on the cross. This is the eternal comfort that only God can give. This is the joy of knowing God as my heavenly Father. The bitterness is the memory, shame, guilt, and sorrow for having offended God. The bitterness of sin is God's means to bring us to seek Him. We become so miserable that we cannot stand to be alienated from God any longer. Once we come to God through the Lord Jesus, the sweetness overshadows the bitterness and gives way to joy unspeakable and full of glory. (See 1 Pet. 1:8.) When we confess our sins and seek God's forgiveness, we realize who we are and how majestic God is. We see the awesome power of His grace, that He would continue to love us and restore and uphold a relationship with us even though we sin against Him. There is a sweet brokenness that accompanies the tears of remorse—the melting and relenting of the soul returning to God—lamenting its former unkindness. "A broken and contrite heart, O God, you will not despise" (Ps. 51:17). This means that God does not despise our brokenness. On the contrary, He delights to embrace a broken heart with His love.

We need to believe the words of promise about repenting of our sin and turning our hearts to God.

> Repent, then, and turn to God, so that your sins may be wiped out, that times of refreshing may come from the Lord.
>
> —ACTS 3:19

But Jesus does not just forgive us. He is as determined to make us holy as He is to forgive us. Titus 2:14 says that Christ "gave himself for us to redeem us from all wickedness and to purify for himself a people that are his very own, eager to do what is good." This was His intention on the cross. He was not only saying, "Father, redeem them, forgive them, pardon them." He was saying as well, "Father, make them holy, purify them, and bring them to a special relationship of loyalty and faithfulness." These characteristics describe a special people who desire more than all else to live near to God and to live according to His Word. May God make us such a people!

> *Father, take my sins, burdens, and my selfishness, and forgive me. Help me to live a life of purity before Your eyes. Enable me to worship You and enjoy Your peace and joy.*

8

WORSHIP AND JOY

Blessed are the people who know the joyful sound!
They walk, O LORD, in the light of Your countenance.
In Your name they rejoice all day long, And in Your
righteousness they are exalted.
—Psalm 89:15–16, NKJV

Have you ever almost worshiped someone, such as a teacher when you were in second grade, the homecoming king or queen, or maybe even a movie star or singer? Though "creature" worship is foolish and wrong, it is often an overwhelming, uncontrollable devotion, even a passion. We would give up everything for that person, and we would do everything in our power to be just like him or her.

Now compare that with worshiping God. It is a much greater relationship than anything we experience with another human being because when we believe in God, we begin to see His power and glory and grace. We behold His countenance, and we are overwhelmed by His majesty. Worship is a summary of our entire response to God, who is the beginning and the end, the Maker of heaven and Earth, our Creator and Redeemer.

Many, O LORD my God, are the wonders you have done.
The things you planned for us no one can recount to you;
were I to speak and tell of them, they would be too many
to declare.

—PSALM 40:5

All things are of God, all things are through God, and all
things are sustained by the breadth of His might. His knowledge is without bounds. His wisdom is infinite. His riches are
immense and inexhaustible. His majesty is awe-inspiring. His
omnipotent power is seen from the galaxies to the mysteries of
a single cell.

The heavens declare the glory of God; the skies proclaim
the work of his hands.

—PSALM 19:1

In Him we live and move and have our being. We open our
eyes and know He is there. He has rained down blessings from
heaven upon the Earth where He has placed us. This rich and
well-furnished world provides all our necessities. While we are
busy spinning in the direction of one year, He is preparing for
another.

God is infinitely above any need that we may have of Him.
He is above our reach. He is above our conceptions; we cannot
comprehend Him. Yet when we surrender our lives to God and
believe in His promises, we find our ultimate existence and purpose in Him.

Once we are in God's presence, we cannot help but worship
His majesty and praise Him. We also cannot help but find joy
in God's grace and power. There is no other way to feel when we
fall at the feet of the Master. We are in awe of the salvation and
fellowship He bestows on all who trust in Him.

Compare this with the beliefs of a group of epicurean and
stoic philosophers the apostle Paul met in Athens. Epicureans

believed it was hopeless to search by reason for pure truth, so they sought true pleasure through experience. Stoics believed in human self-sufficiency and stern self-repression.

They were intrigued by what Paul had to say about Christianity. His words still speak to us today:

> The God who made the world and everything in it is the Lord of heaven and earth and does not live in temples built by hands. And he is not served by human hands, as if he needed anything, because he himself gives all men life and breath and everything else. From one man he made every nation of men, that they should inhabit the whole earth; and he determined the times set for them and the exact places where they should live. God did this so that men would seek him and perhaps reach out for him and find him, though he is not far from each one of us. "For in him we live and move and have our being." As some of your own poets have said, "We are his offspring."
>
> —ACTS 17:24–28

Indeed, the excellency of His nature creates the fires of worship, the desire to praise and glorify Him. Worship is not an end toward something; it is an end in itself. The goal of worship is not to see what we can get out of it; the goal of worship is to exalt God. Worship is gladly reflecting to God the radiance of His worth; it is a spontaneous emotion that genuinely comes from the heart.

Father, You are Lord and You are God. Let me fall at Your feet and worship You as my Maker, Redeemer, and Savior.

LOVE AND WORSHIP

Whatever we love, we praise. Whatever we love, we delight in and enjoy. But this love, this enjoyment, this delight, is incomplete until we can express it. We express our love and delight to God by worshiping Him. He wants us to adore and worship and exalt Him. When we do that, we cannot help but be filled with joy. "I will praise you, O LORD, with all my heart; I will tell of all your wonders," Psalm 9:1 says.

John Piper, in his book, *Desiring God*, calls this joy and pleasure in God, "Christian hedonism."[1] We are satisfied with the excellency of God. We are overwhelmed with the joy of His fellowship. This is the feast of "Christian hedonism"—to be filled with spiritual, godly pleasures.

This "hedonistic" approach is the only humble approach because it comes with empty hands, depending totally upon God for our pleasures and acknowledging that He alone can satisfy the heart's longing to be happy. We love God and are filled with joy at being in His presence.

Jonathan Edwards said religious affections and charity, or love, are the fountain of true religion in the heart.[2] Anything other than that is false. Without this genuine affection and inclination of the soul, religion is dead. We worship God because we love Him and believe His promises.

I start each of my prayers by saying, "Lord, I love You." I want to express the reality that my religion is based in affection. Edwards said, "True religion, in most part, consists of heavenly affections and sensible exercisings of the inclination and will of the soul."[3]

> Then will I go to the altar of God, to God, my joy and my delight. I will praise you with the harp, O God, my God.
> —PSALM 43:4

If we love someone, we treat that person with appreciation, attention, tenderness, and honor. Husbands and wives must love and appreciate each other and care for each other; otherwise, they can get critical, selfish, negative, and judgmental. We must be appreciative in any relationship: with a friend, a coworker, a business partner, or neighbors. It is essential for us to appreciate each other; otherwise, we cannot encourage, praise, intercede for, or love others.

Just as we are aware of the love in our relationships with those who really care for us, God is aware of how much we love and appreciate Him. Our worship of Him parallels how thankful we are for His grace, majesty, glory, sovereignty, and perfect will. From that love and thanksgiving come a constant state of joy, worship, and prayer that permeates us. First Thessalonians 5:16–18 describes this constant state of being:

> Be joyful always; pray continually; give thanks in all circumstances, for this is God's will for you in Christ Jesus.

The times when I am truly able to let all earthly concerns go, I find myself in a "thanksgiving frenzy." It is a time in my relationship with God when I am so filled with joy in His presence that I thank Him for everything I can think of; I am in a state of total abandonment to my faith in Him. I can gauge how close I am to Him and how far away I have turned from my own personal needs. I am no longer wrapped up in myself; I am lifted up into His presence.

I feel closer to God than I do at other times. I just thank Him, knowing my lack and His greatness. He is from the beginning of time and all through eternity, and yet He is at the center of my little life. These thanksgiving frenzies allow me to worship Him in a special way—I do not have to carry a tune or be a great theologian. I simply appreciate the Lord God almighty, who is everything to me.

Now, I cannot experience these thanksgiving frenzies all the time. But I do seek to be constantly in a state of faith, joy, and worship. For example, as I see patients I say, "We're thankful and blessed for the outcome." That reminds me to be focused on the Lord and thankful to Him for whatever happens. I can use various ways to stay focused: simply by saying Bible verses or praying. It is a constant flow of attention to God.

All of us should seek this attitude of faith, joy, and worship. We must make it part of all our life and realize it is the only important thing that we are doing at any time. Whether we are practicing our chosen profession, participating in the activities of our daily lives, or simply kneeling in prayer with no one watching, we need to be focused on God. God has so designed worship that we receive an immense satisfaction from exalting Him. This background of love and worship that meditates on His goodness and His love is essential to a peaceful, abundant, godly, and joyous life! May our hearts accelerate with joy as we pray:

Lord, I stand in awe of Your majesty, Your grace, and Your love. May I always honor You with all my thoughts, desires, and actions and always believe Your promises.

EXALTING AND BEING EXALTED

More than anything the Lord wants from us, He wants us to praise and worship Him and only Him, unconditionally and without reservations. He tells us this in the Old Testament. Speaking to Moses in Exodus 34:14, God said, "Do not worship any other god, for the LORD, whose name is Jealous, is a jealous God."

God said He would tolerate no rivals for the loyalty of the people of Israel. His name, or character, is "Jealous." In the same way, He demands that same kind of exclusive devotion from us. God wants what is rightfully His. How should we respond? Praise should be given to God for who He is, so we lift Him up or exalt Him.

It may seem strange that a God who is supposed to be all-loving wants to be all-exalted. But it is not a vain desire; He wants our worship because He gives Himself back to us when we worship Him. He asks us to exalt Him with everything we have, and with that exaltation we are lifted up. It is like a husband saying to his wife, "Sweetheart, you stick with me, because I am determined to take care of you and bless you!"

God wants us to share in the demonstration of His glory; to enjoy His glory; to give Him glory. Now, it might seem selfish to us that God wants our total devotion, worship, and faith. Yet that is exactly the way it is. It is simply the affirmation of the Creator for the created, and the created for the Creator.

> Yours, O LORD, is the greatness and the power and the glory and the majesty and the splendor, for everything in heaven and earth is yours. Yours, O LORD, is the kingdom; you are exalted as head over all.
>
> *—1 CHRONICLES 29:11*

Jesus told us the greatest commandments are to "Love the Lord your God with all your heart and with all your soul and with all your mind" and "Love your neighbor as yourself" (Matt. 22:37, 39). And while in worldly realms it may appear selfish, in godly terms it is the epitome of unselfishness. Maybe we should call it godly selfishness. In godly selfishness we realize the best thing we can do is worship God and give worth to others. This godly selfishness benefits us, and it benefits others. What we gain is a closer relationship with God, which helps everyone.

Human, or carnal, selfishness is something we maintain solely for ourselves. Godly selfishness is the only way to ascribe worth to God and to others. So, worship is a self-advantageous thing: it not only lifts us up, but it lifts up all the relationships around us.

We can see this in the way we deal with people every day. If we attempt to encourage people by loving them, caring for them, and seeing the good in them rather than looking down on them we are blessed ourselves. A person who spends all day at work trying to be indifferent to people, in effect putting them down, will become that way with a spouse. In the book, *Good to Great*, by Jim Collins, a level five CEO realizes that he is part of something much bigger than himself. The same is true in our walk as a believer.[4]

On the other hand, a person who ascribes worth to coworkers, looking for their best and attempting to pick them up, carries over that attitude to the home and relationships with family and friends.

Our highest good and joy come from keeping our focus on God. True worship is personal, real, and deeply satisfying. Our self enters into the greatest experience of our existence when we worship God.

In any relationship in which two people care about each other, each strives to make the other happier. That is true as we worship God. We want to please Him and exalt Him. And as He is exalted, He cares to make us happy by giving us a closer relationship with Himself.

I once knew a little girl named Felicity. I thought she was beautiful. I am sure when she grew up many men who saw her thought, *My, she would provide a great deal of joy and peace,* which is what the word *felicity* suggests.

However, no person can do that for another. It is empty striving to think we can obtain the Spirit's joy and peace in anything other than our exaltation of God. With our exaltation we accept a pearl of His presence, which is the greatest gift we can receive. That pearl of His presence gives us the fruit of the Spirit—love, joy, peace, patience, kindness, goodness, faithfulness, gentleness, and self-control—that comes from simply praising Him.

Jonathan Edwards sums it up this way in his sermon, "The Unique Excellency of Christ":

In the person of Christ we meet infinite glory and lowest humility. In no other person, do we find this paradox truly perfected. It is His divine nature: the infinitely adorable, and yet with no pride. Christ has the deepest reverence toward God and equality with God. He has infinite worthiness of good and the greatest patience under the suffering of evil. He has exceeding obedience and yet supreme domination over heaven and earth. In Christ is brought together absolute sovereignty and perfect resignation. In Him we see self-sufficiency and an entire trust in God. He has infinite majesty and yet utter humility, to be our servant."[5]

Lord God, as I worship You, change me. Fill me with true humility and love that I may better love You and serve those around me. Work this into my life by the power of Your Holy Spirit.

DUTY OR LOVE?

You crowned him with glory and honor.
—HEBREWS 2:7

Throughout the Bible we are told that we should crown the Lord with glory and honor. God desires honor and splendor to be given to Him given freely in gratitude from our hearts. The joy we experience in worshiping God cannot be experienced in any other act. C. S. Lewis said, "The very nature of Joy makes nonsense of our common distinction between having and wanting."[6] Joy strengthens us in our service and in our work for God.

Let me explain with an example. If I come home on my wedding anniversary with a dozen red roses for my wife and she says, "My, you have these beautiful roses for me. Why did you do it?" Suppose I reply, "I did it because it is my duty. A man should have character and should give his wife roses for their anniversary." Such a response would not go over well. It would not make her heart glad. Nor does it make the Lord glad if we do everything merely out of duty.

Suppose I tell my wife, "Heather, I just want to be with you; I just want to hold your hands and be close to you. These red roses are just a token of how my heart feels—wanting to be as close as possible to you. Let's spend the day together." She would respond very differently to my expression of love than to one of duty. It is not my duty so much that pleases her, but my joy and my honor to be with her.

The Lord also wants our love rather than just our sense of duty. We need to delight in Him and He will give us the request of our heart—namely the satisfaction and joy of the Holy Spirit.

Not long ago Chuck Colson was one of the speakers at a meeting.[7] Chuck is a fabulous Christian and one of the greatest citizens of America today. He expounds the gospel of Jesus Christ in a very courageous way and he is faithful, fervent, and focused.

At this meeting, Chuck gave his usual talk about the duty of Christianity. He is a good lawyer, and he analyzed everything very well, discussing duty to God and country, duty to society, duty to our families, and many other duties that we as Christians need to recognize. He used many Scripture references, including Ephesians 2:10, which is right after the verse stressing that we are saved by grace. "For we are God's workmanship, created in Christ Jesus to do good works, which God prepared in advance for us to do." Chuck Colson is right! We have duties to do in the church.

Immediately after Chuck's talk, a theologian with a much more demure presentation said, "I don't want to disagree with you, Mr. Colson, but I think it's much more important for us to have the joy of the Lord in our heart than for us to be involved in tasks. It's more important that we be filled with God's Spirit."

Believe and Rejoice

The speaker was John Piper, whose books include *The Plea-sures of God* and *Desiring God*. In his books he points out the need for the joy of the Lord within our hearts so we enjoy God in our service as well as in our worship.[8] It is easy for us to jus-tify ourselves by our actions, our tasks: giving money, going to the mission field, "doing" in the name of the Lord. But we really cannot have the joy of the Lord in our hearts until we surren-der to Him, confess our sins, and ask for His forgiveness, which cleanses our hearts.

Many of Piper's thoughts are based on the book *The Life of God in the Soul of Man* by the Reverend Henry Scougal, first published in the 1700s.[9] George Whitefield, an eighteenth-century evan-gelist, said he had finally understood "true religion" is the union of the soul with God, and Christ formed within it, after he had read that treatise.[10]

Scougal points out that we really cannot ever have God's true joy until we have renounced the desire for the things of the world and have released all our resentments. We cannot have the joy of God until we have surrendered our heart and life to Him. We can do all the works in the world, but unless we have His anointing, they do not mean anything.

The Westminster Catechism sums it up this way:

> The chief end of man is to glorify God and enjoy Him forever.[11]

When I first read that statement years ago it seemed like very light reading and simplistic theology. It seemed almost too easy to do. But I have come to understand that God does not want just words of praise. He wants us to commit our lives to worshiping Him with a relinquished heart—one that genu-inely feels His presence in our lives. In this way, relinquishment becomes a joyful surrender and an abandonment of delight in our Redeemer.

Therefore, I urge you, brothers, in view of God's mercy, to offer your bodies as living sacrifices, holy and pleasing to God—this is your spiritual act of worship.

—ROMANS 12:1

When our hearts are relinquished to Him, we hand over control of our lives; we become living sacrifices. This relinquished life is the way we worship Him. And when we praise and worship Him with a relinquished heart, we find true freedom and joy.

Paul wrote:

So that Christ may dwell in your hearts through faith. And I pray that you, being rooted and established in love, may have power, together with all the saints, to grasp how wide and long and high and deep is the love of Christ, and to know this love that surpasses knowledge—that you may be filled to the measure of all the fullness of God.

—EPHESIANS 3:17–19

It is that simple and that profound. Exalt, or worship, God. Enjoy Him. Be filled with joy.

Our tasks are good, but they must be balanced with religious affections. That balance comes with maturity as a Christian; our "ought to's" become our "want to's." It is just as Jesus said:

I have food to eat that you know nothing about....to do the will of him who sent me and to finish his work.

—JOHN 4:32, 34

Dear Lord, help me to submit to You in love. Help me relinquish my heart, mind, and soul to You in the charity that You have given me. Thank You for the joy and felicity that fill my life as I seek to grow in my abandonment to Your promises.

WORSHIP CHANGES US

Praise, love, and enjoyment of God produce in us an everlasting joy as we struggle in a world that is mean and contemptible, that can destroy everything we are and own. All of us have found ourselves encumbered by our worldly lusts. Yet God requires purity and separation from those attitudes, which are constantly seeking to make inroads into our lives.

As we think of God and praise and worship Him, we realize how far short of Him we fall. We grow humble and have the lowest thoughts of ourselves. This is true humility because it results from worshiping God and relinquishing ourselves to Him. It is not something we decide to acquire. It comes from worshiping Him. As our worship becomes all-consuming, affecting every part of our person, humility becomes ours because we are molded by His Holy Spirit that overflows in us. That humility is essential to enjoy God's fellowship, which is the greatest blessing in our lives.

So by desiring true worship, with faith in His promises, above everything else—works, tithing, duties—everything comes into balance. We end up tithing, we end up doing works, we end up "being" before "doing." In our striving to exalt Him, we begin to walk after Him and become more like Him.

> But we all, with unveiled face, beholding as in a mirror the glory of the Lord, are being transformed into the same image from glory to glory, just as by the Spirit of the Lord.
> —2 CORINTHIANS 3:18, NKJV

When we look in an everyday mirror, we see a reflection of ourselves. But this verse refers to a divine image. Paul wrote of the Word of God as a mirror, reflecting to us the Lord Jesus Christ and His glory. We stand in awe and wonder at such a Person, such a Savior, as our Lord Jesus. We behold His glory and want to worship His majesty.

You have made known to me the path of life; you will fill
me with joy in your presence, with eternal pleasures at
your right hand.

—PSALM 16:11

David set before us the reality of a fullness of joy in God's
presence, joy that comes when we behold God's countenance,
when we are caught up in His majesty, and when we relinquish
ourselves. Being in His presence has to change us because it is so
overwhelming.

When we worship His majesty, the Holy Spirit changes us.
We are changed into His image from glory to glory. We must
learn and re-learn every day to put the Lord first, embrace His
promises, serve Him, and take Him as our all in all. Our job is
simply to adore Him and worship Him. Our greatest desire is
that our Maker is pleased. God is infinitely happy in Himself,
and nothing is going to shake or unsettle His throne.

In turning back to God, we cannot take things personally
and internalize them. By internalizing, we change our biology,
our physiology, and our outlook. We change the way we think
and what we become. Instead, we must truly look to the Lord
with a relinquished heart and mind.

One of my friends used to tell me that he needed to pray
earnestly a minimum of forty-five minutes each morning. His
prayers did not make him perfect, but they brought him closer
to God. He had more problems and sins than anybody else
would admit, but he was honest enough to admit his failures.

Like him, I have every distraction in the world. And like
him, prayer brings me back when I abandon myself and exalt
the Lord. That abandonment brings us to a deeper relationship
with God, and a more beautiful tranquility and felicity permeate our whole being. We have an afterglow of peace that is overwhelming. When a person comes together with God in worship,
he personifies a tranquility that is associated with knowing God,

being close to God, worshiping Him in ecstasy, and then having a nature that is changed because of the nearness of God. We become what we pray, and our prayers become the life of God in us. We must be like the Spanish explorer who burned his ships on arrival to America. There is no going back on true dedication and abandonment.

The fire of devotion and adoration must always be kept alive by our attitude when we are active in other things. We should be in such a state of worship that life does not become an effort. It becomes a matter of believing in His promises and relaxing in His felicity. Then our lives are transformed from effort and duty to a state of meditation on the glory of God and willing service from the heart.

The diamonds of God's majesty are needed to plow up a heart as hard as mine. Only then can I receive the seeds that are His precious Word. Only when His majesty truly touches my heart can His Word fill my whole being. Then these seeds will flourish and grow because I believe fully in His promises and respond to Him in worship. No longer do I live with worry or want. I surrender my concerns and desires to Him, and I live a life filled with faith and worship. The jewels of His crown enter my eyes, and I see as He sees. Then He has truly changed me. I see the glory of God in everything and relinquish it all to Him.

> But may all who seek you rejoice and be glad in you; may those who love your salvation always say, "The LORD be exalted!"
>
> —PSALM 40:16

9

A JOYOUS LIFE

Joy is the natural outpouring of our hearts as God's presence becomes the central pillar of our lives. Psalm 16:11 says, "You will fill me with joy in your presence." How wonderful that sounds! When we embrace God as the focus of our hearts, we are transformed. We do not look at ourselves and our lives in the same way. We do not worry about events, we do not long for the things of this world, we do not try to find our ultimate happiness in other people or in our work or play. When we turn ourselves over to God, we cannot help but be joyful, for God is our joy.

C. S. Lewis wrote about this transformation in his autobiography. He said that from childhood he found that he was always longing for something, and he believed that "something" was joy. After his conversion, as he writes at the end of his autobiography, he asks, "What about my search for joy?" His answer: "After I found God, I didn't think much more about it."[1]

Joy is not the product of seeking after joy; it is the product of seeking after Jesus. It is the feeling that comes from being centered on Him and not on ourselves. As C. S. Lewis pointed out, joy is a response to the presence of God's love in our souls. People who seek after true godly joy don't look to themselves; they look to God.[2]

Believe and Rejoice

There is a story about a memory expert who appeared on an interview show. The expert kept calling the interviewer Bob when his real name was Bill. The interviewer tried correcting the guy a couple of times, but he kept calling the interviewer Bob.

This person, who is supposed to understand how memory works, is like many of us, who are supposed to understand the relinquished heart and the joy of relinquished worship. We do not show that joy, we do not show that relinquishment. So we are very much like that memory expert who cannot remember names. We cannot remember to be relinquished and have faith in God's grace. And then our lives do not show the things they should—the fruit and gifts of the Spirit.

Everything in the Bible points out that we must first have a true desire for, and a genuine affection toward, God. When we are focused on appearances, we have a religious spirit. When it comes from within, when our hearts are surrendered completely to God's will, we are filled with joy and felicity.

Dear Lord, may faith in You fill me with Your fruit as You fill my mind with Your Word and presence. Fill my soul with joy as You fill my heart with Your love by the Holy Spirit.

Joy and Laughter

Holy joy is not us trying to build up something within ourselves. It is having a true inner joy. And that joy bubbles out of us in genuine love and laughter.

I once had the opportunity to fish in Alaska with Chuck Swindoll. When we were there, one thing I did in addition to fish was listen to Chuck. And I do not remember a half-hour going by in which Chuck was not laughing. He really laughs!

I have never met a person who laughs as much as Chuck Swindoll. And it is genuine—he is enjoying himself. He has holy joy! He lives Philippians 4:4: "Rejoice in the Lord always. I will say it again: Rejoice!"

All of us should have the joy of God explode within us. We should burst out with joy and laughter.

The son of Abraham and Sarah was named Isaac, which means "laughter" or "he laughs." As an adult, Isaac reopened wells that had been dug in the time of Abraham, which the Philistines had stopped up after Abraham died. Isaac freed up the wells so the water could flow.

In the same way, laughter is important as a way of freeing ourselves up. Frequently we become so serious or so burdened by responsibility that we destroy our ability to laugh, and this damages our ability to be in fellowship with God.

But we should be tuned in to the Person of Jesus, full of the spontaneity of emotion, of laughter, of love, and of caring. Isaac opened up the wells that had been clogged up by the enemy. Those opened wells gave freedom to his people. In the same way, when joined with a joy in the Lord, laughter releases us from the resentment, anger, hate, and bitterness that destroy the spirit. It releases all the stress and anxiety in us and frees us.

Dear God, may my laughter and love come genuinely from You. May my heart be filled with the joy that comes from believing in You.

EXPLOSIONS OF JOY

Finally, brothers, whatever is true, whatever is noble, whatever is right, whatever is pure, whatever is lovely, whatever is admirable—if anything is excellent or praiseworthy—think about such things. Whatever you have

learned or received or heard from me, or seen in me—put
it into practice. And the God of peace will be with you.
—*PHILIPPIANS 4:8–9*

Paul tells us first to think and then to act. Christianity is not
just some theory in our heads; it is in our hearts and in our lives.
When we truly believe and act out the obedience and direction
the Lord calls us to, it is a total experience. There is nothing
greater than knowing the fullness of close communion with the
living God.

Many people have had, or pursued, deeper experiences
with God. These may be physical manifestations of the joy that
comes from being in God's presence. Ultimately, we should
evaluate these experiences according to the Word of God. But
there can be no doubt that some have truly been touched by
God's presence.

Many people throughout church history have been filled
with experiences of joy. For example, John Wesley and his
friend George Whitefield had been having a rough time working for the Lord. So on New Year's Eve, 1738, they bowed in
prayer for twelve hours straight. In this time of prayer they
were completely abandoned to the Lord. They turned everything over to Him. Then, about three a.m., New Year's Day,
a great joy came over both of them. They started singing and
burst forth in a joy that was almost beyond expression. They
were really afraid to tell other people, for fear others would
think they were insane.

Then there was Sarah Edwards, Jonathan Edwards' wife.
(See Appendix IV). She went through a period of spiritual dry-
ness. Then she went into a very deep time of prayer, and she got
what we could describe as "maximum godliness." She developed
an enthusiasm and a joy that caused people to almost think she
was insane. People said she had "distemper and distortion."[3] Jonathan Edwards replied, "If she has distemper, I'd like to have a

little of that distemper. And if she's distorted, the whole church should be distorted."[2] He was very proud that she had exemplified a deeper walk and great godly affection. He thought many who had greater learning and understanding of theology did not feel the affections his wife felt. The understanding without the affection is sterile.

Sarah Edwards felt it was important to keep these experiences in perspective. She described a man who came by to talk about the revival. "Just then Mr. W. came in and with a somewhat light, smiling air spoke of the flourishing state of religion in the town." She could scarcely bear to see him speak in this manner. She thought he was too frivolous. She writes, "It seemed to me that we ought to greatly revere the presence of God and to behave ourselves with the utmost solemnity and humility when so great and holy a God was so markedly present and to rejoice before Him with trembling."[4]

All of us should pursue deep experiences with God, but there is an appropriate manner in which to do so.

Sarah Edwards' words about her own experiences guide us in this:

> My mind was so deeply impressed with the love of Christ and a sense of his immediate presence, that I could with difficulty refrain from rising from my seat and leaping for joy. I continued to enjoy this intense and lively refreshing sense of divine things, accompanied with strong emotions, for nearly an hour. After which I experienced a delightful calm and peace and rest in God until I retired for the night. And during the night, both waking and sleeping, I had joyful views of divine things and a complacent rest of the soul of God.[5]

When we are relinquished to God and feel privileged to be one with Him, that privilege engenders an appreciation that manifests a joy within our hearts. When our laughter is motivated by Christ Himself, we know we have the true balance in heavenly joy.

May the Spirit of grace enable us as we pray:

> *Father, I earnestly seek Your presence in my daily life. Fill me with the tranquility that comes from believing in Your promises. Fill me with intense, lively affections as I am ravished with the beauty of the Son of God— my heavenly Bridegroom.*

CARING FOR OTHERS

When we are filled with joy, we cannot keep it shut up inside us. It has to come out and fill all the parts of our lives and overflow into our relationships with others. We cannot be joyful on the inside, yet cranky on the outside. It will not work. Jesus explains it this way:

> You are the light of the world. A city on a hill cannot be hidden. Neither do people light a lamp and put it under a bowl. Instead they put it on its stand, and it gives light to everyone in the house. In the same way, let your light shine before men, that they may see your good deeds and praise your Father in heaven.
>
> —MATTHEW 5:14–16

We cannot keep to ourselves the love and joy that fill us when we are in communion with God. It pours out of us and onto others. And we are excited to love Him and serve them. Everything that would benefit others makes us rejoice, and we share all of their happiness.

We are no longer filled with self-importance: "If anyone thinks he is something when he is nothing, he deceives himself," Galatians 6:3 warns. Instead, we follow the words of Paul and, with a relinquished heart, put others first:

Do nothing out of selfish ambition or vain conceit, but in humility consider others better than yourselves. Each of you should look not only to your own interests, but also to the interests of others.

—*PHILIPPIANS 2:3–4*

We also find great joy in serving. Psalm 100:2 says to serve the Lord with gladness. The Scottish Metrical Psalms say to serve Him "with mirth." How much easier and more pleasant service is if we do it with mirth and gladness. It is our pleasure, not merely our obligation. And that joy gives us the strength for service—to do the job right.

Remember Mary and Martha? While Mary enjoyed sitting in Jesus' presence, Martha was busy scurrying around getting a meal ready. When we are filled with joy, we are no longer like Martha. We become like Mary in our hearts, focused on Jesus. We can still work hard, but our tasks are done joyfully, out of the desire to do well, not just the need to have things done.

In whatever you do, we need to realize that we are aligning ourselves to God and not just trying to work in our own strength. We are working out of a closeness with God.

As we delight in the Lord Jesus as our chief portion in life, we are enabled to be partakers in the happiness of others—their inward endowments and their outward prosperity.

Lord, let me always find my peace, joy, and rest centered in Calvary. May that peace and joy always be within my heart.

10

JOY AND PEACE

braham was an old man when his son Isaac was born.
God had promised that Abraham would be the father of a
great nation. And after a great trial of waiting, along came Isaac.
Then after a few years, God told Abraham to offer Isaac as a
burnt offering. Can you imagine? Abraham was being asked to
kill his son, his promise of all the future. But Abraham trusted
God. He took Isaac, a knife, and some wood and went up Mount
Moriah, exactly as God had told him.

Notice his response. Abraham did not question God; he sub-
mitted to God's request and promptly did as God asked. He did
not ask others for advice. We do not even know if he asked his
wife, Sarah, Isaac's mother. He worked out all the details of the
trip and set out. And even though it took three days to reach the
place to which God directed him, Abraham still did not doubt
God. In faith, he kept on going, knowing God would provide.

> When they reached the place God had told him about,
> Abraham built an altar there and arranged the wood on
> it. He bound his son Isaac and laid him on the altar, on
> top of the wood. Then he reached out his hand and took
> the knife to slay his son. But the angel of the LORD called
> out to him from heaven, "Abraham! Abraham!" "Here I
> am," he replied. "Do not lay a hand on the boy," he said.

"Do not do anything to him. Now I know that you fear God, because you have not withheld from me your son, your only son."

—*GENESIS 22:9–12*

Abraham was totally abandoned in faith to God. He was totally surrendered to His will. He was willing to do whatever God asked, knowing God would provide the answer.

By faith Abraham, when God tested him, offered Isaac as a sacrifice. He who had received the promises was about to sacrifice his one and only son, even though God had said to him, "It is through Isaac that your offspring will be reckoned." Abraham reasoned that God could raise the dead, and figuratively speaking, he did receive Isaac back from death.

—*HEBREWS 11:17–19*

In one of his sermons, C. H. Spurgeon noted seven blessings that came to Abraham through this trial of his faith.[1] First, the trial was withdrawn and Isaac was unharmed. Second, Abraham received the highest approval of God for not withholding anything from Him. Third, Abraham saw God in a new light, as one who would be willing to sacrifice His own Son, Jesus, for our sins. Fourth, more of God's nature was revealed. He became known as Jehovah Jireh, the God who provides. Fifth, God confirmed His covenant with Abraham because Abraham proved himself faithful at all costs. Sixth, God reemphasized His promise to Abraham about his offspring. "I will surely bless you and make your descendants as numerous as the stars in the sky and as the sand on the seashore" (Gen. 22:17). And finally, God gave Abraham a distinct and personal blessing that has never been repeated.

And through your offspring all nations on earth will be blessed, because you have obeyed me.

—*GENESIS 22:18*

Imagine Abraham's joy as he came down the mountain with Isaac. His soul must have been filled with exultation, triumph, praise, and glory. God did it! God is faithful! Hallelujah! Abraham must have been overwhelmed and full of joy—the joy of worshiping Jehovah Jireh, the God who provides. Abraham did not have to offer his son. The Lord was his provider.

In the same way we must abandon ourselves to God in every circumstance. We must believe in the Jireh half of the Lord's name, Jehovah Jireh. We must believe that the Lord will provide everything!

> When the LORD brought back the captives to Zion, we were like men who dreamed. Our mouths were filled with laughter, our tongues with songs of joy. Then it was said among the nations, "The LORD has done great things for them." The LORD has done great things for us, and we are filled with joy.
>
> —PSALM 126:1–3

This is the joy of abandoned faith. Abraham went up Mount Moriah filled with faith. He came back down the mountain overwhelmed with joy. We can approach the mountains of our own experiences in the same way: up with faith in our hearts, and back down filled with joy.

Recently I was given a copy of a beautiful sermon by C. H. Spurgeon that is more than one hundred years old. It was based on Romans 15:13:

> May the God of hope fill you with all joy and peace as you trust in him, so that you may overflow with hope by the power of the Holy Spirit.

I love how Spurgeon then tied peace and joy together. He said, "Peace is joy resting, and joy is peace dancing. Joy cries 'Hosannah' before the well-beloved, but peace leans her head on His bosom."[2] Peace and joy balance beautifully because they balance on Calvary. There is nothing we can do to force that balance. We must be centered on Christ and Calvary, having faith in Him and not in ourselves.

Two things we see constantly in the early Christians are the love of Christ and joy in Christ. They gave up all their material things, renounced everything that was dear to them, and faced all kinds of suffering.

What happened? Well, the world thought they were crazy. They were imprisoned, tortured, and killed. But that did not stop others from carrying on the mission. The flame of God's truth kept burning brightly.

These early believers had unspeakable joy. They loved God so much that they no longer saw with physical eyes. The pearls of God's majesty were transformed into their eyes, and they saw as God saw, not as the world saw. They saw something unseen—heaven, eternity. They loved Jesus Christ because they saw Him spiritually, and the world saw Him not.

> Though you have not seen him, you love him; and even though you do not see him now, you believe in him and are filled with an inexpressible and glorious joy, for you are receiving the goal of your faith, the salvation of your souls.
>
> —1 PETER 1:8–9

Like them, we can experience a transforming encounter in God's joy and majesty when we fix our hearts and eyes on Him. We can see like He sees, and our hearts can feel like He feels. We can worship Him and become connected to His love and joy. Then we will have true, deeper union and communion with God—in thanksgiving, prayer, service, felicity, rejoicing, and praise.

Jeremiah teaches us one of the indispensable elements of true spiritual joy—the joy that comes from digesting the Word of

God. "Your words were found, and I ate them, And Your word was to me the joy and rejoicing of my heart; For I am called by Your name O LORD God of hosts" (Jer. 15:16, NKJV). God speaks to us by His Word. He works renewed life in us by the creative power of His Word. He revives our joy as we hear His voice in the Word of God as real as His voice from heaven. The Spirit quickens us and we experience true communion with the living God. The practical application we must make is a determination to memorize God's Word. What we do not memorize we will not utilize. We utilize the Word by meditating on it throughout the day, throughout all of our daily activities. We utilize it in prayer and in sharing a word in season with others. In many ways the Word digested causes joy and usefulness to spring up in our lives. Eat the Word like Jeremiah and you will find it the joy and rejoicing of your heart!

Believe, Then We Will Be Enabled to Rejoice

When we truly believe, then we will be able to rejoice with joy both inexpressible and full of glory. True faith is receiving God's Word and resting in His redemption. True faith is hearing the Bible, not as the word of man, but as the Word of God. It is experiencing the reality of Jesus' words:

> My sheep hear My voice, and I know them, and they follow Me.
>
> —JOHN 10:27, NKJV

True faith is person-to-Person dealing with God. Nothing is emptier than a superficial pretense of believing God; to not really have faith as the greatest passion of our heart. True faith includes a humility and repentance that receives Jesus' benediction poured out upon our heads and in our hearts:

Blessed are the poor in spirit, For theirs is the kingdom of
heaven. Blessed are those who mourn, For they shall be
comforted.

—*MATTHEW 5:3–4,* NKJV

When we believe God's promises from the depth of our
hearts the things that God promises become ours. We are forgiven and can hear Him say to us as He did to the man let down
through the roof at Jesus' feet:

Son, be of good cheer; your sins are forgiven you.

—*MATTHEW 9:2,* NKJV

True faith is an inquiring soul that asks, "Lord, do you care
for lepers? Are you willing to cleanse them?" Jesus answers, "I
am willing; be cleansed." By faith we possess the promises of
God and their fulfillments. The broadest, most encompassing
promise of all is:

I will be a Father to you, And you shall be My sons and
daughters, Says the LORD Almighty.

—*2 CORINTHIANS 6:18,* NKJV

This is the same as God saying to Abraham:

I am your shield, your exceedingly great reward.

—*GENESIS 15:1,* NKJV

We can say like Jeremiah, "The LORD is my portion" (Lam.
3:24). Faith hears God say to the soul out of His Word by the
power of the Holy Spirit, "I will never leave you, nor forsake
you...I have loved you with an everlasting love...Fear not, for
I am with you" (Heb. 13:5; Jer. 31:3; Isa. 43:5, NKJV). Is it any
wonder that joy now fills the heart and floods the soul? When
we truly drink these promises in and believe them as true for
ourselves, then we will rejoice. This is the order: believe and
rejoice. Believe and then you will truly rejoice. We are prom-

ised a joy that the world cannot give and the world cannot take away. We are enabled to "rejoice in the Lord always. I will say it again: Rejoice!" (Phil. 4:4), because the forgiveness and new life that we have in the Savior is from Him and cannot be taken away by any trial or difficulty. However, we must believe Him. We must see Him ruling and reigning above all things and trust His sovereignty to work all things for good for those who love Him. Then we can continue to say that the joy of the Lord is our strength (see Neh. 8:10).

The essence of relinquishment and surrender can be summarized in the prayer: *I can't do it without You, Jesus!* We need to die to self until we get to that point. We need what A. W. Tozer called a "divine conquest of the soul."[3] God must bring us to see that we have nothing else to trust in except Him. Everything is in the hands of the Son of God. "The Father loves the Son and has placed everything in his hands" (John 3:35). Now we must say with David, "Into your hands I commit my spirit," and, "My times are in your hands" (Ps. 31:5, 15). This is a great morning prayer of surrender and dependence: *I can't do it without You Jesus!*

Have we been brought to the place where this prayer is the true expression of our weakness and confidence in the Lord's strength? Is this the way we start our day and return to it often throughout the day? This is the Spirit of God at work in us, reviving us, quickening us, and making us more like Jesus who depended totally on the heavenly Father. This is the kingdom of God at work in your life as a believer.

Let us believe, and then we will be able to rejoice. May we believe until we rejoice. *Lord, sustain our faith and strengthen our joy!*

May the mystery, the romance, and the joy of totally abandoning yourself to the grace of God enthrall you with Him both now and forever.

APPENDIX
I

VERSES ABOUT JOY

Here are some verses from God's Word to help us rejoice in the Lord and in His joy.

Glory in his holy name; let the hearts of those who seek the LORD rejoice.

—1 CHRONICLES 16:10

You have made known to me the path of life; you will fill me with joy in your presence, with eternal pleasures at your right hand.

—PSALM 16:11

The LORD is my light and my salvation—whom shall I fear? The LORD is the stronghold of my life—of whom shall I be afraid?

—PSALM 27:1

You turned my wailing into dancing; you removed my sackcloth and clothed me with joy.

—PSALM 30:11

Then my soul will rejoice in the LORD and delight in his salvation.

—PSALM 35:9

But may all who seek you rejoice and be glad in you; may those who love your salvation always say, "The LORD be exalted!"

—*PSALM 40:16*

Then I will go to the altar of God, to God, my joy and my delight. I will praise you with the harp, O God, my God.

—*PSALM 43:4*

Create in me a pure heart, O God, and renew a steadfast spirit within me. Do not cast me from your presence or take your Holy Spirit from me. Restore to me the joy of your salvation and grant me a willing spirit, to sustain me.

—*PSALM 51:10–12*

Blessed are those who have learned to acclaim you, who walk in the light of your presence, O LORD. They rejoice in your name all day long; they exult in your righteousness.

—*PSALM 89:15–16*

The LORD your God is with you, he is mighty to save. He will take great delight in you, he will quiet you with his love, he will rejoice over you with singing.

—*ZEPHANIAH 3:17*

Therefore we do not lose heart. Though outwardly we are wasting away, yet inwardly we are being renewed day by day. For our light and momentary troubles are achieving for us an eternal glory that far outweighs them all. So we fix our eyes not on what is seen, but on what is unseen. For what is seen is temporary, but what is unseen is eternal.

—*2 CORINTHIANS 4:16–18*

That Christ may dwell in your hearts through faith. And I pray that you, being rooted and established in love, may have power, together with all the saints, to grasp how wide and long and high and deep is the love of Christ, and to

know this love that surpasses knowledge—that you may
be filled to the measure of all the fullness of God.

—*EPHESIANS 3:17–19*

Rejoice in the Lord always. I will say it again: Rejoice!

—*PHILIPPIANS 4:4*

Do not be anxious about anything, but in everything,
by prayer and petition, with thanksgiving, present your
requests to God. And the peace of God, which transcends
all understanding, will guard your hearts and your minds
in Christ Jesus.

—*PHILIPPIANS 4:6–7*

Finally, brothers, whatever is true, whatever is noble,
whatever is right, whatever is pure, whatever is lovely,
whatever is admirable—if anything is excellent or praise-
worthy—think about such things. Whatever you have
learned or received or heard from me, or seen in me—put
it into practice. And the God of peace will be with you.

—*PHILIPPIANS 4:8–9*

Be joyful always; pray continually; give thanks in all circumstances, for this is God's will for you in Christ Jesus.

—*1 THESSALONIANS 5:16–18*

APPENDIX
II

VERSES ABOUT WORSHIP

Here are some verses from God's Word to give us greater insight in worshiping the Lord.

Do not worship any other god, for the LORD, whose name is Jealous, is a jealous God.

—*EXODUS 34:14*

Love the LORD your God with all your heart and with all your soul and with all your strength.

—*DEUTERONOMY 6:5*

Glory in his holy name; let the hearts of those who seek the LORD rejoice.

—*1 CHRONICLES 16:10*

Yours, O LORD, is the greatness and the power and the glory and the majesty and the splendor, for everything in heaven and earth is yours. Yours, O LORD, is the kingdom; you are exalted as head over all.

—*1 CHRONICLES 29:11*

I will praise you, O LORD, with all my heart; I will tell of all your wonders.

—*PSALM 9:1*

The heavens declare the glory of God; the skies proclaim the work of his hands.

—PSALM 19:1

Many, O LORD my God, are the wonders you have done. The things you planned for us no one can recount to you; were I to speak and tell of them, they would be too many to declare.

—PSALM 40:5

As the deer pants for streams of water, so my soul pants for you, O God. My soul thirsts for God, for the living God. When can I go and meet with God?

—PSALM 42:1–2

Then will I go to the altar of God, to God, my joy and my delight. I will praise you with the harp, O God, my God.

—PSALM 43:4

Whom have I in heaven but you? And earth has nothing I desire besides you. My flesh and my heart may fail, but God is the strength of my heart and my portion forever.

—PSALM 73:25–26

Look to the LORD and his strength; seek his face always.

—PSALM 105:4

Therefore, I urge you, brothers, in view of God's mercy, to offer your bodies as living sacrifices, holy and pleasing to God—this is your spiritual act of worship.

—ROMANS 12:1

That Christ may dwell in your hearts through faith. And I pray that you, being rooted and established in love, may have power, together with all the saints, to grasp how wide and long and high and deep is the love of Christ, and to know this love that surpasses knowledge—that you may be filled to the measure of all the fullness of God.

—EPHESIANS 3:17–19

Finally, brothers, whatever is true, whatever is noble, whatever is right, whatever is pure, whatever is lovely, whatever is admirable—if anything is excellent or praise-worthy—think about such things. Whatever you have learned or received or heard from me, or seen in me—put it into practice. And the God of peace will be with you.

—PHILIPPIANS 4:8–9

APPENDIX
III

RELINQUISHED HEART
OR RELIGIOUS SPIRIT?

Here are some verses that outline the difference between a relinquished heart and a religious spirit.

FOUNDATION OF THE RELINQUISHED HEART: THE ROOTS OF JOY

The relinquished heart is surrendered to Christ:

> I have been crucified with Christ and I no longer live, but Christ lives in me.
>
> *—GALATIANS 2:20*

The religious spirit is independent:

> Trust in the LORD with all your heart and lean not on your own understanding; in all your ways acknowledge him, and he will make your paths straight.
>
> *—PROVERBS 3:5–6*

The relinquished heart is repentant:

> The sacrifices of God are a broken spirit; a broken and contrite heart, O God, you will not despise.
>
> *—PSALM 51:17*

BELIEVE AND REJOICE

The religious spirit is overconfident and proud:

> So, if you think you are standing firm, be careful that you
> don't fall!
>
> —1 CORINTHIANS 10:12

FOCUS OF THE RELINQUISHED HEART: GOD IS THE SOURCE OF JOY

The relinquished heart is God-centered:

> I have set the LORD always before me. Because he is at my
> right hand, I will not be shaken.
>
> —PSALM 16:8

The religious spirit is self-centered:

> Stop trusting in man, who has but a breath in his nostrils.
> Of what account is he?
>
> —ISAIAH 2:22

The relinquished heart genuinely praises God:

> I will praise the LORD all my life; I will sing praise to my
> God as long as I live.
>
> —PSALM 146:2

The religious spirit pays God lip service:

> These people honor me with their lips, but their hearts are
> far from me. They worship me in vain; their teachings are
> but rules taught by men.
>
> —MATTHEW 15:8–9

The relinquished heart has an eternal view:

> Therefore we do not lose heart. Though outwardly we
> are wasting away, yet inwardly we are being renewed
> day by day. For our light and momentary troubles are

achieving for us an eternal glory that far outweighs them all. So we fix our eyes not on what is seen, but on what is unseen. For what is seen is temporary, but what is unseen is eternal.

—2 CORINTHIANS 4:16–18

The religious spirit is temporal:

Why, you do not even know what will happen tomorrow. What is your life? You are a mist that appears for a little while and then vanishes.

—JAMES 4:14

The relinquished heart follows the major commandment:

Love the LORD your God with all your heart and with all your soul and with all your strength.

—DEUTERONOMY 6:5

The religious spirit is busy following minor rules:

Woe to you, teachers of the law and Pharisees, you hypocrites! You give a tenth [as your tithe]…But you have neglected the more important matters of the law— justice, mercy and faithfulness. You should have practiced the latter, without neglecting the former.

—MATTHEW 23:23

The relinquished heart is aligned to God:

Though you have not seen him, you love him; and even though you do not see him now, you believe in him and are filled with an inexpressible and glorious joy.

—1 PETER 1:8

The religious spirit is aligned to the world:

> Don't you know that friendship with the world is hatred toward God? Anyone who chooses to be a friend of the world becomes an enemy of God.
>
> —JAMES 4:4

FREEDOM OF THE RELINQUISHED HEART: BY THE HOLY SPIRIT, THE POWER OF JOY

The relinquished heart is set on internal attitudes:

> Set your minds on things above, not on earthly things. For you died, and your life is now hidden with Christ in God.
>
> —COLOSSIANS 3:2–3

The religious spirit is set on external actions:

> Since you died with Christ to the basic principles of this world, why, as though you still belonged to it, do you submit to its rules: "Do not handle! Do not taste! Do not touch!"? These are all destined to perish with use, because they are based on human commands and teachings.
>
> —COLOSSIANS 2:20–22

In the relinquished heart, peace is joy resting and joy is peace dancing:

> May the God of hope fill you with all joy and peace as you trust in him, so that you may overflow with hope by the power of the Holy Spirit.
>
> —ROMANS 15:13

In the religious spirit, there is false peace and no joy:

> "Peace, peace," they say, when there is no peace.
>
> —JEREMIAH 6:14

FRUIT OF THE RELINQUISHED HEART: EXPERIENCES AND EXPRESSIONS OF JOY

The relinquished heart is humble:

> All of you, clothe yourselves with humility toward one another, because, "God opposes the proud but gives grace to the humble." Humble yourselves, therefore, under God's mighty hand, that he may lift you up in due time.
>
> —1 PETER 5:5–6

The religious spirit is full of false pride:

> Do not keep talking so proudly or let your mouth speak such arrogance, for the LORD is a God who knows, and by him deeds are weighed.
>
> —1 SAMUEL 2:3

The relinquished heart is filled with life through the fruit of the Holy Spirit:

> But the fruit of the Spirit is love, joy, peace, patience, kindness, goodness, faithfulness, gentleness and self-control. Against such things there is no law.
>
> —GALATIANS 5:22–23

The religious spirit is killed by legalism:

> He has made us competent as ministers of a new covenant—not of the letter [or law] but of the Spirit; for the letter kills, but the Spirit gives life.
>
> —2 CORINTHIANS 3:6

The relinquished heart is patient:

Be still before the LORD and wait patiently for him; do not fret when men succeed in their ways, when they carry out their wicked schemes.

—*PSALM 37:7*

The religious spirit is strangled by worry:

But the worries of this life, the deceitfulness of wealth and the desires for other things come in and choke the word, making it unfruitful.

—*MARK 4:19*

The relinquished heart intercedes for others:

Therefore confess your sins to each other and pray for each other so that you may be healed.

—*JAMES 5:16*

The religious spirit accuses and criticizes:

If you keep on biting and devouring each other, watch out or you will be destroyed by each other.

—*GALATIANS 5:15*

The relinquished heart puts others first:

Do nothing out of selfish ambition or vain conceit, but in humility consider others better than yourselves. Each of you should look not only to your own interests, but also to the interests of others.

—*PHILIPPIANS 2:3–4*

The religious spirit is full of self-importance:

If anyone thinks he is something when he is nothing, he deceives himself.

—*GALATIANS 6:3*

Fuel (Motives) of the Relinquished Heart: Renewing of Joy

The relinquished heart longs for the Word of God:

> My soul is consumed with longing for your laws at all times.
>
> —PSALM 119:20

The religious spirit is complacent and smug:

> He who is full loathes honey, but to the hungry even what is bitter tastes sweet.
>
> —PROVERBS 27:7

The relinquished heart prays with the Holy Spirit:

> I pray that out of his glorious riches he may strengthen you with power through his Spirit in your inner being.
>
> —EPHESIANS 3:16

The religious spirit uses formal prayer:

> These people honor me with their lips, but their hearts are far from me.
>
> —MATTHEW 15:8

Fire of the Relinquished Heart: Majesty of Joy, the Ultimate Joy

The relinquished heart is filled with God's presence:

> You have made known to me the path of life; you will fill me with joy in your presence, with eternal pleasures at your right hand.
>
> —PSALM 16:11

BELIEVE AND REJOICE

The religious spirit knows only cold obedience, the opposite of love:

> If you love me, you will obey what I command.
> —JOHN 14:15

APPENDIX
IV

SARAH EDWARDS, A MODEL OF RELINQUISHED JOY

Though Jonathan Edwards is well-known as the leader of the Great Awakening on the American scene, his wife Sarah is not as well-known. The maxim that behind every good man is a committed woman was never truer than in the case of Sarah Edwards. In defending the Great Awakening to critics who said it was extreme and unbiblical, Edwards used the experiences of Sarah to show the work of God was not only Biblical, but spiritually exhilarating as well. The following account is excerpted from the famous memoirs of Sereno Dwight (one of the descendents of Edwards) written in 1830.*

Dwight gives us an introduction to Sarah's spiritual growth that he appended to Jonathan's memoirs of her life. Sarah's "piety appears to have been in no ordinary degree pure, intense, and elevated, and that her views of spiritual and heavenly things were uncommonly clear and joyful. Near the close of the year 1738, according to the testimony of Mr. Edwards, she was led, under an uncommon discovery of

---

* Jonathan Edwards, *The Works of Jonathan Edwards*, vol. 1 (Edinburgh: Banner of Truth, 1979). Used by permission.

God's excellency, and in a high exercise of love to God, and of rest and joy in Him, to make a new and most solemn dedication of herself to his service and glory, an entire renunciation of the world, and a resignation of all to God. After this, she had often such views of the glory of the divine perfections, and of Christ's excellencies, and at times, for hours together, without any interruption, that she was overwhelmed, and as it were swallowed up, in the light and joy of the love of God. In the summer of 1740, after a new and more perfect resignation of herself to God, with a yet greater fervency, her views of the glory of God, and of the excellency of Christ, became still more clear and transporting. In the following winter, after a similar but more perfect resignation of herself, and acceptance of God as the only Portion and Happiness of her soul, God appeared to vouchsafe to her, for a long period, a degree of spiritual light and enjoyment, which seemed to be, in reality, an anticipation of the joys of the heavenly world (62).

In January of 1742 she experienced even greater nearness to God than previously. She says, "I felt a strong desire to be alone with God, to go to him, without having anyone to interrupt the silent and soft communion" (62).

Under a delightful sense of the immediate presence and love of God, these words seemed to come over and over in my mind, 'My God, my all; my God, my all.' The presence of God was so near, and so real, that I seemed scarcely conscious of anything else (63).

In the course of the conversation, I uttered as the real language of my heart, with great earnestness and emotion

'Hosanna to King David's Son,
    Who reigns on a superior throne.'

And while I was uttering the words, my mind was so deeply impressed with the love of Christ, and a sense of his immediate presence, that I could with difficulty refrain from rising from my seat, and leaping for joy. I continued to enjoy this intense, and lively, and refreshing sense of divine things, accompanied with strong emotions, for nearly an hour (64).

That night, which was Thursday night, Jan. 28, was the sweetest night I ever had in my life. I never before, for so long a time together, enjoyed so much of the light, and rest, and sweetness of heaven in my soul, but without the least agitation of body during the whole time. The great part of the night I lay awake, sometimes asleep, and sometimes between sleeping and waking. But all night I continued in a constant, clear, and lively sense of the heavenly sweetness of Christ's excellent and transcendent love, of his nearness to me, and of my dearness to him; with an inexpressibly sweet calmness of soul in an entire rest in him (65).

For some time as I lay in bed, I felt such a disposition to rejoice in God that I wished to have the world join me in praising him and was ready to wonder how the world of mankind could lie and sleep when there was such a God to praise and rejoice in and could scarcely forbear calling out to those who were asleep in the house to arise and rejoice and praise God (67).

At one point in this revival period she had a visitor come to the house and say "The sun of righteousness arose on my soul this morning before day." Sarah was able to honestly say to him "That sun has not set upon my soul all this night" (65).

One Saturday night she said "I wished to have the world join in praising him; and was ready to wonder how the world of mankind could lie and sleep, when there was such a God to praise, and rejoice in, and could scarcely forbear calling out to those who were asleep in the house, to arise, and rejoice, and praise God (67).

At times she was so weak from adoration of the Son of God that she could not stand and others had to help her or catch her from falling.

Dwight gives us Jonathan's famous concluding impressions that we also should draw from this account. He says, If we "after reading this statement of facts, still regard the preceding narrative as the offspring of enthusiasm, we shall draw our reply from Mr. Edwards himself: *"Now if such things are enthusiasm, and the offspring of a distempered brain; let my brain be possessed ever more of that happy distemper! If this be distraction; I pray God that the world of mankind may all be seized with this benign, meek, beneficent, beatific, glorious distraction!* What notion have they of true religion, who reject what has here been described? What shall we find to correspond with these expressions of Scripture, *The peace of God, that passeth all understanding: Rejoicing with joy unspeakable, and full of glory: God's shining into our hearts, to give the light of the knowledge of the glory of God, in the face of Jesus Christ: With open face, beholding as in a glass the glory of God, and being changed into the same image, from glory to glory, even as by the Spirit of the Lord: Being called out of darkness into marvelous light: and having the day-star arise in our hearts?* What, let me ask, if these things that have been mentioned do not correspond with these expressions; what else can we find that does correspond with them?" (69).

Dwight summarized this account by reminding us that God will reveal Himself to us in heaven in ways that He cannot now because it would be more than mortal bodies and unglorified souls could bear. However He does reveal Himself to His people here below in amazing measures. These divine disclosures are beyond what we can imagine because we still see through a glass darkly. However, "In proportion as an individual is possessed of holiness, so much more near does he come to God, and so much more clear and distinct is his perception of his true character. "If a man love me," says Christ, "he will keep my words; and my Father will love him, and we will come unto him, and make our abode with him" (John 14:23–24, ASV). Such discoveries of the Divine beauty and glory are, therefore, the *promised reward*, as well as the natural consequence, of distinguished holiness.

SCRIPTURE INDEX

Genesis 2:23   12
Genesis 15:1   91
Genesis 22:17   87
Genesis 22:18   87
Genesis 22:9–12   87
Genesis 31:32   49

Exodus 34:14   69, 96
Exodus 34:29–31, 33–35   18

Deuteronomy 6:5   10, 55, 96, 101

1 Samuel 2:3   54, 103
1 Samuel 25:29   58

1 Chronicles 16:10   1, 93, 96
1 Chronicles 29:11   70, 96

2 Chronicles 7:14   61
2 Chronicles 14:11   36
2 Chronicles 16:9   36

Nehemiah 8:10   20, 92

Psalm 9:1   67, 96
Psalm 16:8   52, 100
Psalm 16:11   76, 79, 93, 105
Psalm 19:1   65, 97
Psalm 27:1   32, 93
Psalm 30:11   39, 93
Psalm 31:5, 15   92
Psalm 35:9   8, 93
Psalm 37:3   31
Psalm 37:7   104
Psalm 40:5   65, 97
Psalm 40:16   78, 94
Psalm 42:1–2   56, 97
Psalm 43:4   64, 94, 97
Psalm 51:10   59, 94
Psalm 73:25   28, 97

Psalm 73:25–26   ix
Psalm 81:17   62, 99
Psalm 89:15–16   64, 94
Psalm 105:4   53, 97
Psalm 119:20   105
Psalm 126:1–3   88
Psalm 146:2   100
Psalm 149:4   10

Proverbs 3:5–6   28, 99
Proverbs 13:12   88
Proverbs 14:30   41
Proverbs 27:7   105
Proverbs 28:13   60

Isaiah 2:22   40, 112
Isaiah 43:5   91

Jeremiah 6:14   102
Jeremiah 15:16   90
Jeremiah 15:19   62
Jeremiah 31:3   91

Lamentations 3:24   91

Daniel 4:37   44

Zephaniah 3:17   5, 94

Matthew 5:14–16   84
Matthew 15:8–9   53, 105
Matthew 23:23   56, 101
Matthew 22:37, 39   70

Mark 4:19   42, 104

Luke 9:23–24   12
Luke 10:41–42   40
Luke 15:21   60
Luke 15:23–24   60
Luke 16:19–26   43

John 3:16   ix
John 3:35   92
John 4:14   50
John 4:32, 34   75
John 10:27   33, 90
John 12:24–25   12
John 14:15   105
John 15:9   x
John 15:11   x

Acts 3:19   63
Acts 13:52   20
Acts 16:31   8
Acts 17:24–28   66
Acts 20:21   2

Romans 10:17   15
Romans 12:1   13, 74, 97
Romans 12:2   27
Romans 14:23   61
Romans 15:13   21, 88, 102

1 Corinthians 10:12   100
1 Corinthians 15:9–10   7
1 Corinthians 15:31   13

2 Corinthians 3:6   55, 103
2 Corinthians 3:18   19, 76
2 Corinthians 4:6   18
2 Corinthians 4:10   13
2 Corinthians 4:16–18   45, 94,
    101
2 Corinthians 6:18   91

Galatians 2:20   2, 12, 14, 26,
    32, 99
Galatians 5:15   104
Galatians 5:22–23   27, 103
Galatians 6:3   104

Ephesians 2:8–9   6
Ephesians 3:16   105
Ephesians 3:17–19   75, 95, 98

Philippians 2:3–4   85, 104
Philippians 2:5–8   32
Philippians 3:8–9   14
Philippians 4:4   81, 92, 95
Philippians 4:6–7   30, 95
Philippians 4:8–9   82, 95, 97

Colossians 2:20–22   55, 102
Colossians 3:2–3   102

1 Thessalonians 5:16–18   68, 95
1 Thessalonians 5:24   31

Hebrews 2:7   72
Hebrews 10:23   31
Hebrews 11:17–19   87
Hebrews 13:5   91

James 4:4   13, 102
James 4:14   27, 101
James 5:16   104

1 Peter 1:8–9   89, 101
1 Peter 5:5–6   54, 103

1 John 1:3–4   17
1 John 1:9   61

NOTES

INTRODUCTION

1. Henry Scougal, *The Life of God in the Soul of Man* (Harrisonburg, VA: Sprinkle Publications, 1986).
2. Oswald Chambers, *If Ye Shall Ask*, 1958, as quoted in *Oswald Chambers: The Best From All His Books*, vol. 1 (Nashville: Oliver Nelson, A Division of Thomas Nelson Publishers, 1987), 250.
3. Scougal, *The Life of God in the Soul of Man*.
4. www.ccel.org/e/edwards/affections/religious_affection.html (accessed December 7, 2006).

1: A HEART OF FAITH, A LIFE OF JOY

1. http://www.fbbc.com/messages/miscsayings.htm.
2. C. S. Lewis, *Surprised by Joy* (Orlando, FL: Harcourt Brace, 1956).
3. *Merriam-Webster's Nine New Collegiate Dictionary*, s.v. "Relinquish."
4. www.ccel.org/ccel/wesley/journal.vi.iii.xvi.html.
5. C. S. Lewis, *The Weight of Glory and Other Addresses* (Grand Rapids, MI: William B. Eerdmans Publishing Co., 1965).

2: THE JOY OF SALVATION

1. http://en.wikipedia.org/wiki/sehnsucht_(c._s._lewis).
2. Jonathan Edwards, *The Works of Jonathan Edwards* (Edinburgh: Banner of Truth Trust, 1974).

3: BEING RELINQUISHED

1. Charles Swindoll, *Laugh Again* (Dallas, TX: Word Books, 1992).
2. www.churchlink.com.au/churchlink/worldscope/voice/wesley.htm.

3. Owen Milton, *Christian Missionaries* (Bryntirion, Wales; Evangelical Press, 1995) 69.

4. www.simusic.com/worship/hymns/.

5. C. H. Spurgeon, *Autobiography* (Edinburgh: Banner of Truth Trust, 1962).

6. Tony Evans, *The Fire That Ignites* (Sisters, OR: Multnomah Publishers, 2003), 10.

7. www.maninthemirror.org/alm/alm90.htm.

8. Information available online at http://www.ccel.org/ccel/baxter/saints_rest.pdf.

9. Ibid.

4: TRAITS OF A RELINQUISHED LIFE

1. Earl Palmer, *The Search for Joy*, April 23, 1995, found at www.30goodminutes.org/cses/sermon/palmer (accessed June 8, 2004).

2. James Hudson Taylor (1832–1905), Founder China Inland Mission, biography available online at http://www .wholesomewords.org/missions/biotaylor4.html (accessed 1/05/07).

5: THE STRUGGLE TO STAY RELINQUISHED

1. Aniefiok Udo's story available online at www .fellowshipnashville.org/aoi/index_files/page449.htm (accessed 1/05/07).

6: RELINQUISHED OR RELIGIOUS?

1. Martyn Lloyd-Jones, *Spiritual Depression: Its Causes and Cure* (Grand Rapids, MI: William B. Eerdmans Publishing Co, 1965).

8: WORSHIP AND JOY

1. John Piper, *Desiring God: Meditations of a Christian Hedonist* (Portland, OR: Multnomah Press, 1991).
2. Jonathan Edwards, *The Works of Jonathan Edwards*, vol. 1 (Carlisle, PA: The Banner of Truth Trust, 1990).
3. Ibid.
4. Jim Collins, *Good to Great: Why Some Companies Make the Leap and Others Don't* (New York: HarperCollins, 2001).
5. Edwards, *The Works of Jonathan Edwards*.
6. C. S. Lewis, *Surprised by Joy* (Orlando, FL: Harcourt Brace, 1956).
7. Chuck Colson, Prison Fellowship Ministry, 1856 Old Reston Ave., Reston, VA 20190, email: correspondence@pfm.org.
8. John Piper, *Desiring God: Meditations of a Christian Hedonist* (Portland, OR: Multnomah Press, 1991) and *The Pleasures of God: Meditations on God's Delight in Being God* (Portland, OR: Multnomah Press, 1991).
9. Henry Scougal, *The Life of God in the Soul of Man* (Harrisonburg, VA: Sprinkle Publications, 1986).
10. Nigel Clifford, *Christian Preachers* (Bryntirion, Wales; Evangelical Press, 1994) 161.
11. *The Westminster Larger Catechism*, 2002, found at www.reformed.org/document/larger1.html (accessed June 1, 2004).

9: A JOYOUS LIFE

1. C. S. Lewis, *Surprised by Joy* (Orlando, FL: Harcourt Brace, 1956).
2. Ibid.
3. Paraphrased from *The Works of Jonathan Edwards*, Vol. 1 (Carlisle, PA: The Banner of Truth Trust, 1990).
4. *The Works of Jonathan Edwards*, Vol. 1 (Carlisle, PA: The Banner of Truth Trust, 1990).
5. Ibid.

10: JOY AND PEACE

1. C. H. Spurgeon, *Autobiography* (Edinburgh: Banner of Truth Trust, 1962).
2. Ibid.
3. A. W. Tozer, *The Divine Conquest* (Old Tappan, New Jersey: Fleming H. Revell Co., 1950).

ABOUT THE AUTHOR

James P. Gills, M.D., received his medical degree from Duke University Medical Center in 1959. He served his ophthalmology residency at Wilmer Ophthalmological Institute of Johns Hopkins University from 1962–1965. Dr. Gills founded the St. Luke's Cataract and Laser Institute in Tarpon Springs, Florida, and has performed more cataract and lens implant surgeries than any other eye surgeon in the world. Since establishing his Florida practice in 1968, he has been firmly committed to embracing new technology and perfecting the latest cataract surgery techniques. In 1974, he became the first eye surgeon in the U.S. to dedicate his practice to cataract treatment through the use of intraocular lenses. Dr. Gills has been recognized in Florida and throughout the world for his professional accomplishments and personal commitment to helping others. He has been recognized by the readers of *Cataract & Refractive Surgery Today* as one of the top 50 cataract and refractive opinion leaders.

As a world-renowned ophthalmologist, Dr. Gills has received innumerable medical and educational awards. In 2005, he was especially honored to receive the Duke Medical Alumni Association's Humanitarian Award. In 2007, he was blessed with a particularly treasured double honor. Dr. Gills was elected to the Johns Hopkins Society of Scholars and was also selected to receive the Distinguished Medical Alumnus Award, the highest honor bestowed by Johns Hopkins School of Medicine. Dr. Gills thereby became the first physician in the country to receive high honors twice in two weeks from the prestigious Johns Hopkins University in Baltimore.

In the years 1994 through 2004, Dr. Gills was listed in *The Best Doctors in America*. As a clinical professor of ophthalmology at the University of South Florida, he was named one of the best Ophthalmologists in America in 1996 by ophthalmic academic leaders nationwide. He has served on the Board of Directors of the American College of Eye Surgeons, the Board of Visitors at Duke University Medical Center, and the Advisory Board of Wilmer Ophthalmological Institute at Johns Hopkins University. Listed in Marquis' *Who's Who in America*, Dr. Gills was Entrepreneur of the Year 1990 for the State of Florida, received the Tampa Bay Business Hall of Fame Award in 1993, and was given the Tampa Bay Ethics Award from the University of Tampa in 1995. In 1996, he was awarded the prestigious Innovators Award by his colleagues in the American Society of Cataract and Refractive Surgeons. In 2000, he was named Philanthropist of the Year by the National Society of Fundraising Executives, was presented with the Florida Enterprise Medal by the Merchants Association of Florida, was named Humanitarian of the Year by the Golda Meir/Kent Jewish Center in Clearwater, and was honored as Free Enterpriser of the Year by the Florida Council on Economic Education. In 2001, The Salvation Army presented Dr. Gills their prestigious "Others Award" in honor of his lifelong commitment to service and caring.

Virginia Polytechnic Institute, Dr. Gills' alma mater, presented their University Distinguished Achievement Award to him in 2003. In that same year, Dr. Gills was appointed by Governor Jeb Bush to the Board of Directors of the Florida Sports Foundation. In 2004, Dr. Gills was invited to join the prestigious Florida Council of 100, an advisory committee reporting directly to the governor on various aspects of Florida's public policy affecting the quality of life and the economic well-being of all Floridians.

While Dr. Gills has many accomplishments and varied interests, his primary focus is to restore physical vision to patients and to bring spiritual enlightenment through his life. Guided by his strong and enduring faith in Jesus Christ, he seeks to encourage and comfort the patients who come to St. Luke's and to share his faith whenever possible. It was through sharing his insights with patients that he initially began writing on Christian topics. An avid student of the Bible for many years, he now has authored nineteen books on Christian living, with over eight million copies in print. With the exception of the Bible, Dr. Gills' books are the most widely requested books in the U.S. prison system. They have been supplied to over two thousand prisons and jails, including every death row facility in the nation. In addition, Dr. Gills has published more than 195 medical articles and has authored or coauthored ten medical reference textbooks. Six of those books were bestsellers at the American Academy of Ophthalmology annual meetings.

As an ultra-distance athlete, Dr. Gills participated in forty-six marathons, including eighteen Boston marathons and fourteen 100-mile mountain runs. In addition, he completed five Ironman Triathlons in Hawaii and holds the record for completing six Double Ironman Triathlons, each within the thirty-six hour maximum time frame. Dr. Gills has served on the National Board of Directors of the Fellowship of Christian Athletes and, in 1991, was the first recipient of their Tom Landry Award. A passionate athlete, surgeon, and scientist, Dr. Gills is also a member of the Explorers Club, a prestigious, multi-disciplinary society dedicated to advancing field research, scientific exploration, and the ideal that it is vital to preserve the instinct to explore.

Married in 1962, Dr. Gills and his wife, Heather, have raised two children, Shea and Pit. Shea Gills Grundy, a former attorney and now full-time mom, is a graduate of Vanderbilt University and Emory Law School. She and her husband, Shane Grundy,

M.D., have four children: twins Maggie and Braddock, Jimmy, and Lily Grace. The Gills' son, J. Pit Gills, M.D., ophthalmologist, received his medical degree from Duke University Medical Center and, in 2001, joined the St. Luke's practice. "Dr. Pit" and his wife, Joy, have three children: Pitzer, Parker, and Stokes.

THE WRITINGS OF JAMES P. GILLS, M.D.

A BIBLICAL ECONOMICS MANIFESTO
(With Ron H. Nash, Ph.D.)
The best understanding of economics aligns with what the Bible teaches on the subject.
ISBN: 978-0-88419-871-0
E-book ISBN: 978-1-59979-925-4

BELIEVE AND REJOICE: CHANGED BY FAITH, FILLED WITH JOY
Observe how faith in God can let us see His heart of joy.
ISBN: 978-1-59979-169-2
E-book ISBN: 978-1-61638-727-3

COME UNTO ME: GOD'S CALL TO INTIMACY
Inspired by Dr. Gills' trip to Mt. Sinai, this book explores God's eternal desire for mankind to know Him intimately.
ISBN: 978-1-59185-214-8
E-book ISBN: 978-1-61638-728-0

DARWINISM UNDER THE MICROSCOPE: HOW RECENT SCIENTIFIC EVIDENCE POINTS TO DIVINE DESIGN
(With Tom Woodward, PhD)
Behold the wonder of it all! The facts glorify our Intelligent Creator!
ISBN: 978-0-88419-925-0
E-book ISBN: 978-1-59979-882-0

THE DYNAMICS OF WORSHIP
Designed to rekindle a passionate love for God, this book gives who, what, where, when, why, and how of worship
ISBN: 978-1-59185-657-3
E-book ISBN: 978-1-61638-725-9

EXCEEDING GRATITUDE FOR THE CREATOR'S PLAN: DISCOVER THE LIFE-CHANGING DYNAMIC OF APPRECIATION
Standing in awe of the creation and being secure in the knowledge of our heavenly hope, the thankful believer abounds in appreciation for the Creator's wondrous plan.
(Hardcover) ISBN: 978-1-59979-162-3/ 978-1-59979-155-5
E-book ISBN: 978-1-61638-729-7

BELIEVE AND REJOICE

GOD'S PRESCRIPTION FOR HEALING: FIVE DIVINE GIFTS OF HEALING
Explore the wonders of healing by design, now and forevermore.
ISBN: 978-1-59185-286-5
(Hardcover) ISBN: 978-0-88419-947-2
E-book ISBN: 978-1-61638-730-3

IMAGINATIONS: MORE THAN YOU THINK
Focusing our thoughts will help us grow closer to God.
ISBN: 978-1-59185-609-2
E-book ISBN: 978-1-59979-883-7

LOVE: FULFILLING THE ULTIMATE QUEST
Enjoy a quick refresher course on the meaning and method of God's great gift.
ISBN: 978-1-59979-235-4
E-book ISBN: 978-1-61638-731-7

OVERCOMING SPIRITUAL BLINDNESS
Jesus + anything = nothing. Jesus + nothing = everything. Here is a book that will help you recognize the many facets of spiritual blindness as you seek to fulfill the Lord's plan for your life.
ISBN: 978-1-59185-607-8
E-book ISBN: 978-1-59979-884-4

RESTING IN HIS REDEMPTION
We were created for communion with God. Discover how to rest in His redemption and enjoy a life of divine peace.
ISBN: 978-1-61638-349-7
E-book ISBN: 978-1-61638-425-8

RX FOR WORRY: A THANKFUL HEART
Trust your future to the God who is in eternal control.
ISBN: 978-1-59979-090-9
E-book ISBN: 978-1-59979-926-1

THE PRAYERFUL SPIRIT: PASSION FOR GOD, COMPASSION FOR PEOPLE
Dr. Gills tells how prayer has changed his life as well as the lives of patients and other doctors. It will change your life also!
ISBN: 978-1-59185-215-5
E-book ISBN: 978-1-61638-732-7

THE WRITINGS OF JAMES P. GILLS, M.D.

THE UNSEEN ESSENTIAL: A STORY FOR OUR TROUBLED TIMES...
PART ONE
This compelling, contemporary novel portrays one man's transformation through the power of God's love.
ISBN: 978-1-59185-810-2
E-book ISBN: 978-1-59979-513-3

TENDER JOURNEY: A STORY FOR OUR TROUBLED TIMES...
PART TWO
Be enriched by the popular sequel to *The Unseen Essential*.
ISBN: 978-1-59185-809-6
E-book ISBN: 978-1-59979-509-6

DID YOU ENJOY THIS BOOK?

We at Love Press would be pleased to hear from you if

Believe and Rejoice

has had an effect on your life or the lives of your loved ones.

Send your letters to:
Love Press
P.O. Box 1608
Tarpon Springs, FL 34688-1608